Where the Trail Grows Faint

Where the Trail

River Teeth Literary Nonfiction Prize

SERIES EDITORS

Daniel Lehman
Ashland University

Joe Mackall
Ashland University

The *River Teeth* Literary
Nonfiction Prize is awarded
to the best work of literary
nonfiction submitted to the
annual contest by *River Teeth:
A Journal of Nonfiction Narrative.*

A Year in the Life of
a Therapy Dog Team

Grows Faint

LYNNE HUGO

University of Nebraska Press
Lincoln & London

© 2005 by the Board of Regents
of the University of Nebraska
All rights reserved
Manufactured in the
United States of America
⊗
Library of Congress
Cataloging-in-Publication Data
Hugo, Lynne.
Where the trail grows faint : a year in the
life of a therapy dog team / Lynne Hugo.
p. cm.
ISBN 0-8032-2432-X (hardcover : alk. paper)
1. Dogs—Therapeutic use. 2. Older people—
Rehabilitation. 3. Human-animal relationships.
I. Title.
RM931.D63H84 2005
615.8'515–dc22
2004024174

For Alan, my partner on the trail

Contents

Author's Note

The names of the nursing facility, residents, and staff have been changed because I went there not to write a book, but to give service with my dog. *Where the Trail Grows Faint* began with a journal kept while I was working on another manuscript. As residents and staff opened themselves to Hannah and me, neither they nor I were aware that their stories would eventually find their way into a book. Many vulnerable people shared themselves without reservation, and I feel a responsibility to make public my indebtedness and gratitude but keep their identities private. In two cases I have also changed identifying physical details.

Where the Trail Grows Faint

1. First, Everybody Leaves You

"Hey! Is my husband here?" demands an ancient woman in a wheelchair as I'm searching for the activity coordinator who will orient me as the first animal-assisted therapist in the Golden View Nursing Home. I've signed in, draped matching purple photo IDs around Hannah's neck and my own, and skirted two patients parked near the receptionist's window because my dog is already making a fool of me. I take her aside for a little chat about her behavior, but Hannah's obedience training has apparently been deleted and she's got enough pull on the leash to dislocate my arm. Now she thinks she's going to climb into this patient's lap.

"Hannah, dammit, quit that!" I hiss, not the exactly correct command, but I'm getting a little rattled.

No matter. The old woman hasn't noticed. She's scrunched her eyes beneath her forehead, a low-slung storm cloud, to better peer into the distance behind me. I hoist Hannah back and say I'll go find out about the missing husband. But the old woman cuts me off, flipping her wrist dismissively in front of her own face.

"Oh no. He's dead," she answers herself nonchalantly. Recovering the fact seems to cheer her. "What's that you've got there?"

I'm pleased by the question, of course. This is what we're here for, my trusty trained dog and I. I square my shoulders and answer proudly. "This is Hannah. She's a Labrador retriever. This color is called chocolate. Would you like to pat her?"

As she considers, the cheer disappears. "I don't know. Dogs are complicated."

"You don't need to take care of her. You can just pat her if you like."

"Is it a boy dog or a girl dog?"

"She's a girl."

"Oh. The boys are even more complicated."

I am undeterred. "Men can be like that, can't they? But this one's a girl. Much easier. Would you like to pat her?" A pause, then a negative head shake. "Still too complicated. He's dead, you know, my husband. Sooner or later they leave you. First thing you know, everybody leaves you." Another dismissive wave in front of her own face, and she will not speak again.

This job is not going to be as easy as I thought. I'm not ready after all. Hannah's not ready either. Who cares what tests we've passed? Training for this already appears as helpful as classes for fish on how to ride a bicycle. I remind myself that just yesterday Hannah and I hiked an unfamiliar section of forest where mounds of fallen leaves were so deep as to obscure the trail, if there even *was* a trail. I'd had no choice but to follow my instincts . . . and my dog.

The first day I met her, it's a good thing I didn't know I'd ever have to follow Hannah anywhere because I'd have panicked. An eggbeater on a trampoline might have been less in motion. I wanted a good look at the ten-month-old chocolate Labrador retriever we were adopting, but Hannah's greeting involved bouncing four paws off my torso while administering an exuberant French kiss. I squatted to aim a calming hand at her collar only to be knocked the rest of the way over and given a face, neck, and ear bath. "You don't get out much, do you girl?" I gasped, a canny observation of the exquisitely obvious.

Our feisty fourteen-year-old cockapoo had died. We'd loved Peaches and, against advice, kept him although we were constantly warning people—or apologizing to them—about his snapping. My closest friend has had Labs for years and my family had grown attached to old black Shadow and pup Betty, watching Shadow's muzzle gray and her gait falter by arthritis until the summer they had to put her down. But through years of trail hiking with Barbara and our dogs, I'd seen the reliability of the Labs' friendliness, their eagerness to please, the sweetness of their tolerance.

My husband, Alan, and I contacted the coordinator of a regional Lab rescue organization, a woman who takes in endangered or stray Labs, giving them medical care and remedial loving until she can find a family who is a good match. Hannah needed a home and attention;

we wanted a young, people-loving, female Lab. "I have the perfect dog for you," Carol said when she called.

"This is an exceptional puppy without an aggressive bone in her body and equally without an ounce of training," she enthused through the phone. "She's spent an inordinate amount of time alone, muzzled so she won't cry and get the young woman who owns her evicted from a no-pets apartment. She's finally realized that much as she wants to keep Hannah, she just doesn't have the time or the place to meet a Lab's needs. She was going to donate her for training as a Seeing Eye dog, but she's called Lab Rescue instead because she thinks Hannah would be happiest if she can run and swim and play with other dogs and people, have a home like yours, if you get my drift. You're perfect for her. And she's perfect for you." Carol definitely hadn't said anything like this when we'd discussed other dogs, all of which had had some problem that gave me pause.

So I went to pick up this dog for whom we were so perfect, who was so perfect for us.

Ah yes. Perfect with one small exception. Hannah absolutely hated to be left home alone as I discovered when I went to the post office the next morning, a fifteen-minute trip which cost me one black dress shoe. The Puppy Retaliation-For-Being-Alone Diet for the first month included but was not limited to: one silk tree (expensive), numerous house plants (African violets in bloom preferred), my reading glasses, one bottle of Oil of Olay (made her coat nice and shiny), one Chapstick (made her lips . . . etc.), one framed picture of my daughter (who'd apparently annoyed Hannah by returning to college), twenty-four foil-packaged FiberBars (produced enough gas to power a small city), two double batches of brownies left to cool on the kitchen counter by some slow learner, one Birkenstock sandal, and a roll of toilet paper (assumed necessary after the brownies incident). The financial damage in the first week or so approached the cost of purchasing a Westminster Best of Show dog, and I thought we'd been tricked into adopting the devil's protégée. Plus, people staggered under the onslaught of her greeting; I was afraid she'd eventually overtax the local ambulance system.

In retrospect the obvious question flashes in neon: why on earth didn't we crate her? I have no excuse for such stupidity except that we were overly eager to make her happy and were also convinced that once she began getting exercise (the first owner had had no place to run her, and she was about ten pounds overweight as a result) she'd settle down. We were correct in that assumption. Sort of.

We began serious training. Hannah was brilliant in obedience school, one of two dogs who passed Level II and the American Kennel Club (AKC) Canine Good Citizen Test out of nine who'd been in that intermediate class. People still staggered under the onslaught of her greeting, but she'd sit nicely afterward. And her distaste for solitude continued unabated; even now, leave her alone and she's not above chowing down a roll of paper towels or amusing herself by removing all the little appointment cards and notes stuck to the refrigerator. Her *coup de grace* was eating the first obedience diploma she earned, displayed there like the children's report cards used to be. And she seemed to enjoy the Christmas lights she took down for us, although unfortunately she didn't wait until the season was over.

Meanwhile, I was falling in love. I found myself saying things like, "I'll be back, Sweetheart, I promise," ad nauseum every time I had to leave the house however briefly. When I started taking her with me— not because she'd still be upset at being separated but because now *I* would—I knew it was all over. I have no idea how the first owner found the strength to give her up. It was an extraordinarily unselfish thing to do. I thanked and blessed her daily from the storehouse of gratitude Hannah's presence created in me. And I never forgot her first notion, that Hannah, this beautiful animal of long-tongued kisses and earnest work to please, would be an ideal service dog, because she was absolutely right. I'd been the recipient of such a gift that sharing her, giving service with her, seemed the right thing to do.

Most dog owners' faces soften with pleasure—with love—when they're asked about their animals. They think their dogs are unique in temperament, intelligence, perception. So I'll probably sound like other dog people when I claim that Hannah is remarkably suited to being a therapy dog, but it's the truth. For one, I've never heard her growl. She approaches all creatures from insect to human with interest, affection, and trust. As open-hearted and consistent as Labs generally are, Hannah has one extra trait making her an extraordinary dog for this work: a sense of humor. She cavorts with an eye to the audience, then stands back and absorbs their laughter like applause, her waving tail a flag of self-satisfaction.

As Hannah starred in ongoing advanced obedience classes with Alan, I applied to Therapy Dogs International (TDI), an organization that certifies teams to work in institutions like hospitals, nursing homes, special schools, and prisons, places where we know people benefit from direct animal involvement. First, the dog must pass the AKC intermediate obedience test and be approved by a vet, then be tested by a TDI animal evaluator on obedience skills again as well as the ability to work around medical equipment and to tolerate clumsy patting, restraining hugs, startling noises, and sudden movements. (The Delta Society has extremely similar requirements—along with a lengthy training manual and video on which the handler is tested. Both organizations provide insurance for the handlers of the animals they evaluate and accept, as well as photo IDs, special collars, and tags.)

Hannah had already earned the AKC obedience title before we applied. Given her innately affectionate nature, it didn't take much more work before she trotted through the TDI certification test, and I thought we were ready. I might have been a bit delusional, but that's what I thought.

Carla, the activity coordinator, has worked in the nursing home since she was fifteen. In her mid-thirties now, her experience as well as kindness shows in the respectful yet intimate affection with which she approaches the residents. She knows these people. They are touched often by business hands: aides who bathe, dress, and feed them, physical therapists, and even doctors, who come once a month to certify their ongoing need for care. Carla, though, touches them when it's not necessary and with pure affection. She calls each by name, hugging her way through the quadrangle of halls to introduce us. It's all we're going to do this first day: acclimate Hannah to the facility and see which patients react with the most interest and enthusiasm to the dog. When she first said this, I was disappointed. Now I'm practically faint with relief. It takes an hour to make it down just the first hallway, so many have wanted to talk to Hannah, to touch, caress, play with her, tell her animated stories about their lost pets. Hannah has reciprocated with eager kisses and multiple lap-climbing attempts. This dog definitely does not have a problem with shyness.

Carla tells me she began here at fifteen as an aide, moved to Georgia when she married, then moved back, and back to work here, when she divorced nine years ago. Her own mother died of brain cancer in room A-4 two months ago. "She really didn't suffer," Carla muses. "Considering what I've seen over the years, I dreaded that. I would have given anything to spare her. At least I could have her here, with me."

"But she *was* spared, you say." I insert this a little too eagerly, thinking of my mother and my constant worry about her future.

Carla flips back her long dark curls with a circular head motion. Brown-eyed and petite, she's a woman whose hair style and figure reveal exactly what she looked like at seventeen. "Yes," she says, her voice a soft alto lightly sugar glazed, a country twang. "It was quick. And I was with her every day."

How can I possibly do that for my parents, be there every day? In their mid-eighties, they refuse to move; I have my family and work in this town, 742 miles away. My sister is, likewise, almost 800 miles away. My mother has begun falling with increasing frequency. The parallels between her health and that of the residents here is uncomfortable and unavoidable. The burden is squarely on my father, though Jan and I get there as frequently as we can. The idea of either of our parents in a nursing home is anathema to us. But what *will* we do? Every one of my baby boomer friends who has living parents is at war with the same question.

Even this new to the nursing home, I can see what an issue it is here: the heart and time of relatives to assist in care and provide companionship. At least 50 percent of the 120 residents of this facility spend the bulk of their day slumped in wheelchairs parked in the hallway, staring into their own laps. Some areas show that an effort has been made to decorate and personalize them—just now Santa Claus cut-outs and tinsel are omnipresent enough to put an elementary school to shame—but I cannot shake the sense that old people, suffering old people, are warehoused here like excess boxes when the attic is full and nobody knows what to do with them anymore.

Of course, even heart and time aren't enough. Distance can cancel both before they're even revved up. Right now my favorite uncle is two thousand miles away from his closest surviving birth family as he lies dying of lung cancer in California. He's the fifth of my father's seven younger siblings to be eaten alive by the disease. I still see him as he was when I was ten and he was rakish in military khakis, teasing me, always teasing, but all my life, though I've gone for years at a stretch without seeing him, ending every phone conversation with, "I love you, sweetheart." Only morphine mutterings remain now. He is diapered, on his deathbed, and I will not hear him say it again.

How quickly life shifts, too, as if cosmic fingers snap and, unless proximity has made a decision for us, at once we're called upon to decide how much heart and time we have, no matter how ill prepared we are, how unexpected the crisis. A week ago, Hannah took off after a deer, disappearing from a trail in the nature preserve where we hike daily, most often with Barb, and her black Lab, Betty. That particular day, Barb's husband, aptly named Hardy, was with us. We three slogged through an icy December rain calling, calling, calling. Tall and fit at sixty-five, Hardy strode at a steady clip, his thick thatch of straight steel gray fallen over his forehead. The uneasy results of a cholesterol test notwithstanding, there was no way there was anything wrong with that man's heart. But within days, he'd have an angiogram and be kept in the hospital for a quintuple heart bypass operation then and there, and I'd spend the night at the hospital with Barb awaiting the surgeon's verdict. Sometimes we lose people quickly, sometimes cell by cell, and sometimes there's a reprieve, and we don't think about losing again until we must. But I think about it all the time now, composing new verses to the baby boomer blues while I sing the refrain in concert with my whole generation.

And there's the agenda I'd prefer to ignore. I'm past fifty. Do I imagine myself in a nursing home? Not in this lifetime. My husband just brought home information on long-term care insurance and I didn't put it in the trash. I put it in the shredder. Yet my genetic history and health habits suggest I may live long enough to need it.

Today, Hardy is in intensive care, two days post surgery. My uncle is dying and my parents are both scheduled for cataract removal, one tomorrow and the other next week. Dad has a crop of new skin cancers that must come off quickly; he's already had one bad biopsy that required surgery, just after Mom's first serious fall, the one that broke her shoulder. All of it feels connected, as Hannah and I start work at the nursing home, in a December that's warmer than anyone has a right to expect.

Carla finally gives up trying to introduce us to everyone she has in mind. Our progress is far too slow. Everybody wants time with Hannah, and that includes the staff members who tag along to play with her while they tell sad and funny stories about their dogs. Finally, I just have to go. Barb is at the hospital, and I must pick up Betty and exercise both dogs before dark.

My fleece jacket is enough for our hike, gloves jammed, unnecessary, in the pockets. The trail is brighter now that the hangers-on leaves have let go, and afternoon light is a pale, gilt wash over the woods at three, though dark will be early and long. Except for the startle of red berries on the honeysuckle, I could mistake the afternoon for early spring. I could mistake how the season holds its breath and think it indecisive between winter and summer, as if it could go either way.

I stop streamside and hold my own breath, as if I, too, could go either way or just wait, here, while I hold what I love and lose nothing more. Of course, it is scarcely a minute before Hannah and Betty, who'd run ahead to the creek, bound back to see what's holding up their swim. Betty drops a tennis ball at my feet and Hannah rushes in to steal it, as she always does, wanting to be the one to perform on the "Drop it, girl" cue. And the dogs and I move on, the suspended moment unrolling into time.

2. A Velvet Anger

Outside, a brilliant clarity of sunlight. Since my first visit to Golden View, we've had a deluge of snow followed by a thaw that has softened the air to a mimic of late March. Only the remaining snow, really, and the foreshortened afternoon already suggesting early twilight, insist January. The light scarcely penetrates to the nursing home, though. There's a darkness that hangs from the ceiling and clings to the walls like fog, though at least it's odorless. All of the rooms are doubles, hospital-like, and I am struck by how few of them are individualized with pictures or plants or the hand-knit afghans I associate with my parents' generation. Or perhaps that was my grandmothers' generation and what I remember were hand-me-downs to begin with, long relegated to a Goodwill box by whomever cleaned out the attic of the family home before it was sold.

I sign in and get a blank stare from a chubby thirty-something receptionist. The same two patients ("Call them *residents*," Carla said, but I keep forgetting) are parked in the reception area. One is a very heavy, really hugely heavy, woman whose age I can't guess, fair-skinned, pink-cheeked, dark-eyed, near-black bunned hair circled by a hot-pink scrunchie. She waves one fist but I can't tell if it's spastic or a deliberate greeting until she speaks. I make out, "Come here, baby. Come here, baby," from a longer, slurry string of words.

Hannah manages to drag me to the wheelchair. I am scarcely thwarting her determination to leap into the sloping lap when Carla happens in from the far side and calls, "Hey, Connie, how're ya doin'?" neatly supplying me with a name. Connie flails at her lap, urging Hannah up as I'm trying to hold her down. Trying, and losing, that is. Now Connie's wheelchair begins rolling backward thanks to Hannah's scrambling. I stutter an apology as Carla scurries to rescue all of us. But Connie's giggling.

Carla gives me a list of the residents she'd like me to see. Although he's new to Golden View, the name of my eighty-three-year-old next-door neighbor, Peter, isn't on it, doubtless because he isn't speaking much and doesn't remember that he loves dogs. At his own home, though, he and his wife, Helen, still have the very same yellow Lab they got from my sister twelve years ago. Jan's dog had puppies right when they needed one, and she put Dawn on a plane to them. Sometimes now Peter doesn't remember Helen, let alone Dawn. I detour to his room as I start Carla's list, but he's so soundly asleep I cannot rouse him. Helen's told me he'll be up, agitated, all night. The staff thinks he has his days and nights confused, but she believes he's overmedicated. She fears he'll be cheated out of his chance for phys-ical and occupational therapy. Already he's missed his turn several times because they couldn't wake him up. It's a big issue because he's only allotted two weeks to show he's "making progress" on the much more expensive rehabilitation floor, according to Social Security standards; "progress" earns more time. Lack of it gets him moved to a regular room. Hannah licks Peter's hand, which doesn't twitch a response any more than the kiss I put on his forehead.

Hannah and I head down the corridor to the half room Carla's favorite resident, Mary, has made distinctly her own. Her narrow bed has been arranged as if the curtain that divides the room is a wall. Her back to the roommate's area, Mary faces the one window on the back wall upon wakening. A crucifix and an embroidered sampler of the Serenity Prayer, a leftover palm from some past Easter season stuck in its wooden frame, must be the first objects she sees in the morning. Or maybe she sends her eyes to the window to absorb the sky itself. She has a crocheted afghan folded neatly at the foot of the bed, over a bright patchwork bedspread. Framed pictures of grandchildren cover the two walls to the left and right of the bed. A small television set is on a table in front of the window. Magazines, several books, china dog knickknacks, an African violet. Here is a world reduced to six feet by eight.

Today her roommate isn't there and Mary is sitting in an uphol-stered chair, sun spilling over her, as she works a crossword puz-zle. Immaculate and groomed, she wears a lavender striped blouse, matching lavender skirt, hose and tie shoes. She's tiny, her white hair slightly wavy, parted to the side and combed back neatly.

"Mary, may I come in?" I say, Hannah again ahead of me, straining the leash. (She's now in the advanced level at obedience school and never pulls stunts like this in class. Training a therapy dog in the field is apparently just a tad more tricky than I'd grasped.)

I asked Mary's permission to enter because it feels intrusive to me not to. How little privacy or personal space the residents have. Essentially anyone can barge in any old time, and it seems they do. It would make me completely crazy in short order.

"Well of course, of course," she says, surprised at the question.

There's no place for me to sit except in Mary's wheelchair or on her bed. The wheelchair seems the better choice. Hannah is nosing up to Mary and as soon as Mary reaches to pat her, Hannah ducks and goes over the reaching hand with a neck and tongue stretch of Guinness-record length. Mary gets her chin washed. "Oh my, oh my," she says, but she's chuckling and brushes my apology aside.

Without my asking, Mary begins telling her story. "I've lived here for ten years, since I was eighty," she says. "And I do everything, I take care of myself. They don't like it, but that's the way I want it. My husband and I came here together and four months later he died, his heart, you know, and I just stayed. When we came, they said we could have a room together, but they put us in different rooms. They said it was because he wanted me to take care of him and it would be too much for me. Balderdash! I *wanted* to take care of him and I *could*. I would have asked for help when I needed it." She looks away, out the window. "They kept us apart. After he died, I'd thought I'd go to my son's but . . . well, I had to stay here instead."

My mind won't wrap around this. She's healthy-looking. Frail, but no more so than my mother. Surely if she can take care of herself in a nursing home, she could do well in assisted living, or, indeed, at her son's. But some mystery surrounds the topic. "The doctor wanted me to stay," she says at one point, which makes no sense to me, given the current insurance climate. Her blue eyes redden around the periphery and I come to realize this is what I'll see when she's crying. "Everybody's gone," she says. "I don't know why I'm here. I don't understand. I'm ready to go. Why does God leave me here? What the hell is He thinking?"

There's a *lot* of religion in the nursing home. Religious services and bingo are the big activities and lots of words about faith and God's plan fly up and bounce off the ceiling like corn being popped. And I know it's sincere. Still, the edge of bitter anger in Mary's voice is unmistakable.

"When you think about that, do you come up with any possible answers?" I ask softly. The rims of her eyes, which had reverted to normal, redden again.

"No," she says, "not one. Maybe He's just a moron. It's not like I'm doing any good here."

When Henry David Thoreau lay dying, a family member asked, "Henry, have you made your peace with God?"

"I didn't know that we had quarreled," he answered.

Mary not only knows she's quarreled, she feels she's owed one big apology. Yet her relationship with God is so large in her life, so intimate, that she presumes the right to refer to Him disparagingly.

Maybe to divert Mary out of the melancholy, staring silence into which she lapses, I pass her Hannah's bag of treats. Hannah rouses from her stretched-out nap on the linoleum at the slight, crinkling-bag sound and, chronically starving, snarfs them out of Mary's palm. Mary nestles each side of Hannah's face with her hands. "Oh, I love you, girl," she says. "I love you. There were some kittens here once, but people complained. Another time we had a puppy but that staff member left and the puppy went with her. They all leave. But I'm still here."

Her son, who lives less than four miles away, comes to see her once a week. Mary thinks he is wonderfully attentive. Her eyes go red around the rims again when she adds, "I'm used to being alone. Everybody leaves. That part doesn't really bother me." She says this without rancor.

I hurry to make it out on time after I finish my rounds, but Barb and I miss each other. Literally. She'd thought we were hiking the dogs at three, but I arrive at four thirty, the earliest I could have gotten there. When I get to the trail entrance, her Jeep isn't there, so I wait in the parking area while Hannah prances, impatient to get going. Finally I realize there's been a miscommunication somewhere and I'll have to go alone.

I already know there won't be others out with their dogs today. Barb and I are diehards who ignore the weather, but there aren't many of us. It's a dank, cold day, tiny ice needles falling, forming a white skim over the trails. The muddy ruts our boots left in the first winter thaw are firming up in this new cold spell and hiking is manageable again without the sucking pull of sodden earth. Barb has left a couple of big notes scratched in the snow. *Hannah*, she directs with an arrow at a fork in the trail, mocking my assertion that Hannah can read, so I know she's been there and gone already. She must have thought I might be shortly behind her and could catch up. Her footprints, and Betty's, are the only disturbances on the earth's new frosting.

Once I walked alone regularly but not so often now. What would it be like if my husband were gone, my parents, Barb, and my sister, too—if I had no friends, no co-workers, no neighborhood with a shared history? If I couldn't have my dog? I try to stretch my mind to encompass Mary's length of loneliness, but I can't come close. Yesterday Hannah ate the twenty-eight birthday candles I'd laid out for my son's birthday cake, snagging them off the kitchen counter while I made a run to the post office. I suppose that's one way to stop time.

"Get that dog out. You can't have that dog in here." A wizened woman, dwarfed in her wheelchair, accosts me in the hall just after I sign in. I haven't been coming for enough weeks to be thrown out, not yet anyway. Hannah is getting the hang of wheelchair etiquette and hasn't managed to roll Connie backward down a flight of stairs during the tongue-bath greeting. Okay, so there aren't any stairs here, but Hannah really *has* behaved.

"Oh yes, Ma'am. It's really all right. See? I'm supposed to be here." I lift the ID badge I've just put on and point to Hannah's with my other hand. "And so is she. She's a special dog, trained. We're from . . . uh . . . well, some residents really miss their pets, you know, and this is a special program so they can have one." I'm going to have to work on my pitch: that last part is sort of a lie. I'm the whole program. Although there *are* nursing homes filled with live plants, animals, birds and children ("Edenizing" facilities), this definitely isn't one of them.

I expect an argument. "Oh," she shrugs. "Well, bring her over here so I can pat her." She can't remember the breed of the dog she had. A sidelong eye beads on me. "Don't laugh," she warns, though I'm sure I haven't made that mistake. "You'll get old. You won't remember either. I'm ninety-five."

Later on, when I'm introducing Hannah to Theresa, who says dogs scare her but she wants to try touching one, the old woman spins herself in abruptly.

"Australian shepherd," she declares and executes a snappy about-face to wheel herself away.

Meanwhile, Theresa is shaking her head. "It's easy to forget things. I forgot that a baby wasn't mine." She's strapped into a wheelchair, and I'm trying to put some food in her hand so she can feed Hannah—always instantly anyone's best friend when there's food in hand—but Theresa can't make her hand cooperate. "It's paralyzed," she says, pointing at it with her chin.

"Did you have a stroke?"

"No. They don't know what's wrong with me. Just one day my legs wouldn't work. Then I had a lot of tests, and they couldn't find a single thing wrong with me."

"Was this after you forgot the baby wasn't yours?"

Theresa teared. "Well, that was because it was my daughter's, but she left it with me so long I thought it was mine. Then she came and I wouldn't let her have it because I thought it was my baby. Shoulda been. I went to the hospital for a week, but then they let me out so's they could arrest me for stealing the baby. She wouldn't let me see the baby for a long time after that. But now I can be out of jail as long as I say it's her baby. My daughter still don't want much to do with me. Mad, I guess. That's why they put me here."

"And then your legs . . . ?" As if on cue, Hannah begins nosing Theresa's knees, which makes her smile.

"Just one day I woke up and couldn't move them. Then it moved up and up and now it's pretty much everything below my neck. My kids think I'm doing it on purpose, that I'm not really paralyzed. But I am. They just can't find out what's wrong."

Theresa strikes me as a careworn fifty-something that a hard life has aged to look closer to seventy. Ragged gray hair is a wild aura, and her pale face is lined beyond the years her voice suggests. Her eyes still remember blue, but most of the color seems leached out until they resemble her shapeless gray sweatsuit. She tells me she can't recall why she's so afraid of dogs. I can see she likes Hannah, and I keep reshaping her slack hand to hold a few pieces of kibble. Hannah snuffles them out from the loosely curled fingers, and Theresa smiles. "I'll come by next week," I promise when I really do have to go.

"Please. I'd like that," she says, then adds in a conspiratorial voice, "Don't tell them, okay? It's my baby. God forgive me for lying. Do you think that's why He paralyzed me, for lying? But it won't do that baby no good for me to be in jail."

"Theresa, I honestly don't think that's the way things work. I'm glad you're not in jail." I have no idea if this is a good answer or not. I often don't. It's an opinion, mine, given with a hand, mine again, on her shoulder, and it's the human caring that accompanies the dog. I just have to hope it's all right.

I've nearly made it to the exit when a woman with long auburn hair fastened off her face literally runs down the hall calling, "Wait! Wait! May I see the dog?" Her flowing-sleeved white blouse, black slacks, wooden bead necklace and earrings, low-heeled black mules, an artsy professional outfit, leads me to assume she's a staff member, one of the more professional ones at that.

I stop, of course, and she catches up, kneels and hugs Hannah. "I adore dogs," she says. "I've always had them. Do you know Kuvasz?"

I so *don't* know Kuvasz that I'm not even sure she's speaking English.

We have to move aside to let an aide pass pushing a wheelchair. "You might have seen them in a dog show. Big? Long-haired? Usually white . . . *big* . . . stand about this high?" she persists, indicating shoulder height on herself. Several ambulatory patients have, meanwhile, stopped to pat Hannah who is now straining against her training collar ignoring a *sit* command as valiantly as a dog who's never been in obedience class number one. I'm trying to prevent her from knocking over and tongue drenching a hunched and wrinkled resident on a walker as I maintain a semblance of eye contact with the auburn-haired woman, and it's not a graceful picture. "Don't know the breed," I confess, panting harder than Hannah, "never been to a dog show."

"Oh, they're beautiful dogs, quite large. Would you like to see a picture?"

I agree, mainly to escape the hallway where I'm now the queen of a significant traffic jam. I'm expecting she'll lead me to an office, but instead we head into one of the resident rooms, to the bed by the window. "Home," she says sardonically as she makes a sweeping gesture. "Welcome to everything I have left in the world." The decorating attempt and the sheer amount of *stuff*—books, shoes, pictures, random clothes, bead-making projects—crammed floor to ceiling in tottering piles of hopeless disorganization suggests that she's been here quite a while. "I'm Liz," she continues as she removes a picture of a dog that's indeed fluffy, white, and *big* from a bulletin board covered with snapshots. "And this is a Kuvasz."

I pretend to admire the picture but am really trying to orient myself to the discovery that Liz is a resident. This woman is maybe fifty, give or take five years. She's my age, and she's down on the floor playing with Hannah in a very relaxed manner, just as I do. I can see she's probably trained dogs; her touch is expert, confident, and she uses commands easily and correctly.

"Thank you so much for letting me see her. I so miss my dog . . . it's terrible."

"Is he at home?"

"When they put me here, they gave him away," she says, tearing. "He's someplace in down South now. It's a rare breed, very valuable."

"How long have you been here?"

"Two years, three months, seventeen days. But who's counting?" Then she anticipates the question I wasn't going to ask. "Depression."

"Do you have a family?"

She snorts. "Used to, but they're the ones who stuck me in this place, so. . . ."

"Is it helping you to be here?" I *want* them to have a loving motive, and I want her to know it, as if that will ensure my parents' understanding if my sister and I ever have to "stick" one or both in such a place. I'm careful not to think about how I'll understand if my children stick *me* here.

An elaborate shrug. "Nothing changes. You know. They leave you here, out of sight, out of mind. Works for them."

An aide calls Liz to supper. I go out into the world to be with my family, the same family in which grown children routinely kid about having me declared incompetent. One of my son's favorite teases is how he's going to find me "a real nice ol' folks home, Ma, don't you worry your head none. And nuthin' gonna keep me from visitin' right regular, every Christmas, no matter what."

We exit the main doors of Golden View out into weather that blows fresh with inevitable change, the puppy leashed but straining hard toward the future. Of course, Hannah knows full well that the most immediate future holds our before-dinner hike in the woods, and she whines her tail-thumping excitement from the back seat. For me these miles we do together are immeasurably important; time to immerse myself in the otherworld of forest and river and let the day slide from my shoulders trusting that what is valuable will remain in silent presence. Incapable of subterfuge, Hannah is my guide to the heart of experience. She leads me into the dimension of life represented by the nursing home and she leads me back out. In that, I doubt I'm much different from other dog people. But everyone finds his or her own route to life's core, if they look for it and get lucky.

For the nursing home residents as for my parents, the miles before sleep involve no distance, yet the greatest endurance of all as they travel a trail ever more faint. Looking for purpose, extracting meaning, coaxing out joy: these have become our tasks as Hannah and I journey with them.

3. One Dear Voice

At the nursing home, I am always reminding myself that one of the best things Hannah and I can do is to be a mirror in which patients may see the lifelong core of themselves again. Talking about who they were and still are inside lights a revival fire that warms them and holds back the dark. It probably shouldn't surprise me how often my dog, with her silky ears and eager tongue and shiny, caressable coat—the sheer young physicality of her—coaxes out their buried selves, the selves they were when they were in charge of their lives and bodies and spent their time with people of their own choosing. Prompted by Hannah, they begin with a story about the dogs they loved and that single thread often becomes whole cloth.

Clare is a bedridden MS (multiple sclerosis) victim whose speech is affected according to Carla, who asked me to see her and added that Clare's been in the same room, in the same bed, for nine years. Today on her eighty-sixth birthday—exactly my mother's age—a pink carnation corsage is pinned on her sleeveless nightgown and a bouquet of helium-filled latex balloons is tied to one of the raised bedrails. The head of the bed is cranked up to about forty-five degrees. Clare's round face is edged with yellow-white hair that's pulled straight back, as if in a ponytail or bun. What surprises me when I get closer is the very long braid lying on the pillow to one side of her head, a small pink bow tied about half-way down. Bedclothes are tucked neatly over her breasts, flaccid arms left out on top. She's listening to a book on tape. She tried to stop it when we entered, Hannah straining ahead on the leash (we're still working on that pesky heeling stuff), but her hand waved wildly and ineffectively, as if with a separate mind. I stop the tape for her but when she begins to vocalize, my mind seizes with dread that I won't understand her. Background noises—televisions (two to a room, always on, always on different channels), another patient's voice wailing at a continuous, high decibel out in the hall, the loudspeaker through which staff are summoned to the phone—all compete. To focus on one patient's labored effort to communicate seems doomed.

And conversation with Clare requires the real work of sustained attention. Her speech is halt and slurry. When I hear her though, really *hear* her, I recognize a cultured woman with an inner self she can still call forth.

She loves dogs, she tells me, and when I realize that she's not at an angle at which she can see Hannah sitting in the eighteen inches between her bed and the wall, I ask if she'd like me to put Hannah's front paws up on the bed. She would. Her left hand swings and bats like an errant flyswatter when she tries to pat Hannah, who retreats in alarm. Raiding my arsenal of treats, I lure her back up and when the aimless hand starts, I take it in mine and direct it to Hannah's head and ears while Hannah demolishes the food. Now I've got Hannah wedged up between my body and the bed and, though the treats are gone, Hannah's trapped. It's my first experiment in creating canine accessibility, only the first of many, I already see, as there are wheelchairs to approach at the right reach, to say nothing of walkers and the sheet-covered giant beanbag seats in which some patients sprawl in the common area.

"So soft." Clare breathes the words out.

"Isn't she? Feel her ear." Putting Clare's thumb on top of it and forefinger underneath, I slide them the length of the flap. She may not balk at anything, but it's equally true that Hannah's not patient with this quiet detailing for long. Still puppy and still inexperienced here, she wants to play, she wants to do tricks and earn treats, and now she pulls her head away to check my hand for food. At least I *hope* it's a matter of age and experience.

"So soft," she whispers again. "I had a golden retriever. Got him for my tenth birthday. So sweet, even when he got arthritis. Loved him like crazy, used to tell him my secrets. Still miss him, his good company." As she's talking, I space out some kibble on the blanket over Clare's thighs, and Hannah noses them out. Then, ever hopeful, she snuffles around Clare's hand, fallen inert at her side now. Clare's face softens into a soft, nostalgic smile. "Good pup."

"Did your family give you the corsage and balloons?"

A negative head shake, slight. "No. From the facility."

"Oh. Will you see your family tonight, then?"

"My daughter might come. It depends on how her work goes. She doesn't have much time." Whole sentences seem to take too much out of her, and Clare resorts to fragments when she needs to regather energy. "You? Children?"

"I have two. A son in Indiana and a daughter in . . . well, right now she's in South Africa."

"Student?"

"A senior in college."

"I've never been to Africa. I love Europe, though. My daughter is going to Florence for a month. That's a beautiful city. The sculptures, those narrow stone streets. But I love Switzerland, hiking in those mountains. Sweet air and cool. Clean. Snow on top all year. Peaceful." This much takes perhaps two minutes for her to get out, and it's somewhat distorted in the coming. It's possibly as tiring to pick and sort through the sound for discrete words as it is for her to speak them, and I wonder to myself if it's why her daughter doesn't come often.

Wailing starts up again out in the hall. "*I . . . told . . . John . . . no . . . no . . . no.*" The high pitched screech-moan is anguished, desolate. Clare rolls her head and looks into the hallway.

"The Fire Engine Lady," she says. "It goes on night and day. Alzheimer's. Shouldn't be here, should have a separate wing. My opinion."

"It must bother you. Would you like me to close your door?"

Clare starts to answer but at that moment her roommate jerks the drawn curtain between their beds aside with such force that Hannah and I are both startled witless. We'd not even known for sure anyone was in that bed at the moment, but we definitely do now. A woman—the sign outside the door said her name is Edwina—tiny, wizened, with electric-shock hair, starts an incoherent shout. Then she squints at Hannah, shakes her head and stops.

"Oh. You ain't her. I thought you was Lucy again. She was in here before bothering me."

"Gosh, I hope the dog didn't scare you." (*My* heart is pounding double time, which I believe I hide nicely.)

"Oh that ain't nothing. I ain't afraid. Lucy was just in here," Edwina interrupts to confide.

"Lucy?"

"She ain't right in the head. Came in here and said this here is her quilt," she says, fingering the print coverlet on her bed, which looks like it came from a nice department store. "I told her she was a goddamn liar."

"Oh. Um. Is Lucy a patient?"

"She lives here. She ain't right in the head."

Edwina looks to be all of four feet tall, slight and weak, judging from the exertion she's expending to talk. She's wearing a delicate knit sweater, apricot-colored, with ribbon trim, that fine pastel yarn and stitching of a hand-knit baby sweater.

"Goodness. Did you call a staff member to help?"

"No I did not." Edwina says it haughtily. "I take care of my own problems. I'll beat her goddamn ass, that goddamn liar."

With this pronouncement, she reaches for the curtain and with improbable strength flings it closed again.

I catch Clare turning her head to hide a grin.

"The Fire Engine Lady comes in here to argue with Edwina?" I ask Clare dubiously, sotto voce.

"Oh no. The Fire Engine Lady just yodels and chants. It's *Lucy* that comes in here when the staff isn't watching. I'll tell you, some days I'd give anything for quiet, to hear just *one* voice that I *want* to hear. And I'd like to hear my own mind," Clare says. Hannah's tail thumps against the wall like a knock just then and Clare chuckles. "Oh, there it is now . . . trying to escape again."

It's only hours later on the same day that I'm surrounded by the great silence of a furiously falling snow in the woods at twilight. Enormous flakes frost every branch, every bit of ground, rich and thick as if the sky were a goose-down comforter torn open. Clare is on my mind as I take the path to the area Barb and I call the Cathedral. I want the deep white hush of snow on evergreen. Clare's longing for quiet has put me in mind of how I am bothered by constantly blaring televisions, too. With a start, I realize I'm projecting myself into Clare's bed, into her life, and the thought makes me feel trapped and crazed and afraid for the future.

The main trail splits and one snakes uphill, looping away from the river through mature growth deciduous forest to a vast stand of enormous white pines planted in rows like pillars. The trail becomes its wide center aisle, worn in by hikers. Planted in the fifties as a Christmas tree farm, the trees were never harvested. A change of plans left them to grow on, ever higher, thinned only by age and weather. Now, they tower like a Gothic church above a fifty-year carpet of fallen needles. With trunks close enough that there are virtually no lower branches, the tops are a good seventy-five feet overhead, a vaulted cathedral ceiling. Breeze makes them whisper like the breath of God, answering the wood when it moans and creeks. Barb and I have ruled that we may not complain about anything, not even husbands, as we pass through. Instead we recall a sacred moment in our lives when our spirits were grateful and aware.

Hannah and I are virtually soundless as the snowy woods swallow us. She bounds ahead, exuberant, snow settling on her back and tail and tongue as quickly as she shakes it off. Quartering, sometimes ranging off down a game trail, she returns (not always instantly, big surprise) in response to a whistle and a shouted command of "Trail!" though the scent lure is strong. Out here, she is all animal instinct, less bonded or tied to me, and I glory in her power even as her separateness makes me a little sad.

Suddenly, about twenty feet ahead on the long hill that precedes the Cathedral, where there's not much underbrush beneath the old hardwoods, two deer startle and take off, white flags high as they cross in front of us. Hannah flattens into a gallop and gives chase. She doesn't even go into the high-pitched barking frenzy that usually signals she's treed some squirrel that's taunting her from a low branch; these deer are tantalizingly close and she's hoping she'll actually close in on them. They will, of course, quickly outrun her and she's chased enough to know that; yet she can't pass up the chance to open out in that full, fresh run. Such utter physical freedom, such exultation to release in so much unwalled space. I wonder if Clare remembers running as she lies confined, longing for some forest she loved as I do this one, a forest in which the silence was this vast and alive and she could hear one dear voice she *wanted* to hear.

4. Regret

Herman wasn't on any list Carla gave me. Hannah picked him. We were on our way to another room, in fact, when we heard, "Come here, doggie, here, here, doggie," from a source I couldn't identify. Hannah, who never needs a second invitation, tracked it down right away. She turned around and wagged her way into Herman's room to kiss the hand balled uselessly in his lap. I've made sure to see him each time I've been there since that day. Often his is the first room we go to after I sign us in and Hannah tongue-mauls Connie. ("Come here, my baby. Baby, baby, come here," Connie croons, and Hannah is hot to comply. At least I've learned to lock the wheelchair in place.)

Today, as usual, Herman is parked alone in his room. His is the side closest to the window—and the heating unit. It takes less than thirty seconds for sweat to break out on my face and neck. The temperature must be a hundred degrees. Herman, in a long-sleeved plaid flannel shirt, seems to find it quite comfortable, while I immediately shed my sweater and perversely wonder whether his eyesight is bad enough that I could get away with taking off my shirt, too. His glasses are so thick I'm amazed they stay up. Hannah is eyeing the open Twinkies package on Herman's bedside table, but she heeds my hissed warning to "*Leave it*!"

Each time I come, Herman tells me the same two stories. Forty some years ago he had a little blond cocker spaniel that he loved "too much." The cocker ran out onto Highway 27 in front of his house and was killed by a truck. Herman dug a grave in his yard where he buried his friend, painting a big rock to mark the spot. The rock sits there still. Herman could never bear to have another dog, to risk that grief. The story frightens me, loving Hannah "too much" as I do, and knowing it.

The second story also makes him cry each time he tells it. "That's my wife," he always says, pointing to a picture of a young brunette, a deep wave in her shining hair dipping over her forehead as she rests her chin on her folded hands. She wears a small hat with a cloud of fine veil. My mother wore hats like that when I was a child. The portrait looks to have been hand-colored in oil paint, a process pre-dating color photography, I assume. I'm sickened, in fact, by suddenly remembering my own high-school graduation picture, the framed version, "individually hand-colored in oils." I'd had to specify my hair and eye colors on the order form, and I toyed with lying about both in order to be a green-eyed blonde, but finally decided my parents might notice if my graduation portrait looked nothing like my usual shades-of-reddish-brown self.

"She's beautiful," I say, meaning it. It could be a picture of a Hollywood starlet in the 1940s.

"She's been gone for eight years," he says in his raspy voice as he tosses the soft fleece ball I've brought so patients can play with Hannah without risk. Hannah retrieves and drops the ball in his lap. Herman laughs and then immediately starts crying, caressing Hannah's ears with his good hand. Tears run out from underneath those weighty glasses; he wipes his jaw line with his sleeve, but doesn't bother with the rest.

"You miss her a lot."

He nods. "Once I was supposed to take her to town, to the department store. Two thirty in the afternoon, she said, that's when she wanted to go. But, I went and played pool with my buddies and clean forgot about the time. Well, I might have been sort of flirting with some women there. About four thirty I remembered and drove my truck home. Drove way fast. And when I pulled into the driveway, there she was, all dressed up for town and sitting on the porch. When she saw me, she stood up and went into the house and slammed the door. Wouldn't talk to me for a long time."

"She forgave you, though . . ." I venture.

Herman tosses Hannah's ball again and again. "I don't think so," he says. "Next day, I took her to the department store. I gave her all my money and said to get whatever she wanted."

"But you still don't think she forgave you?"

"I just feel so bad," he says, shaking his head to indicate *no*. He takes off his glasses to wipe his eyes. It's awkward to do it all one-handed: remove the heavy glasses, set them down, use the tissue, throw it away, replace the glasses, and I can see why he gives up and just swipes his chin most of the time. He cries often, and sometimes, too, the glasses are fastened to his head, which makes it even more complex.

"There must be a hundred stories about wonderful things you did for her," I say, trying to shift his focus.

"Oh yeah. Yeah. But I just feel so bad about that time."

After we leave Herman, Hannah and I head down the hall and into a common area we must cross to get into the wing where Mary's and Clare's rooms are. We're waylaid though, by Big Sam, a heavy, bushy-haired man in a wheelchair who looks to be in his sixties. His red shirt is the luminous focal point in the large open room; gray mist hovers close to the ground outdoors and whatever natural light there is inside today is shrouded and somber. Big Sam's face lights up when he sees Hannah.

"Hey, pretty doggie, hey come over here."

I nudge Hannah toward where he is parked. She nuzzles the hand he stretches in her direction and he laughs, deep and hearty. It's not a nursing home sound.

"Do you want to give her a treat?"

"Sure. I love dogs."

I hand Big Sam a couple of dog biscuits. "Make her work for them," I caution. "She knows all the commands."

"Sit, girl," he says and Hannah, ever hot for a snack, instantly tucks and plops. Guffaws from Big Sam.

"Shake hands." I tack on the extra command and start to bend over to take Hannah's paw, but Sam outdoes me. He leans so far out of his wheelchair I'm afraid he'll pitch out headfirst, takes Hannah's paw for the shake, and gives her the biscuit. I hand him her fleece ball and he tosses it in the air. She jumps off her hind legs, springing straight up to snatch the ball just as it starts back down. Sam keeps tossing the ball; Hannah keeps grabbing it from the air and depositing it in his lap. Neither shows any signs of tiring of the game after multiple repetitions.

I have Hannah do a little show for him, putting her through a whole range of commands and he's duly impressed. "Had me a dog once," he says quietly, his mood shifting. "I loved that dog. Little poodle it was. Well, sort of toy size I guess." Suddenly he is crying. "Never did have me another dog."

"Why is that?" I say it softly as I hand him a tissue. He may ignore the question, of course. Usually when residents don't want to talk about something, they pretend they didn't hear the question and suggest I chalk it up to "these damn hearing aids."

Not Big Sam, not now. "My mother would never let me, and afterwards I just heard her voice in my head and couldn't. See, the whole family loved that little dog. One time in the summer I was about twelve, I was driving our big tractor mower. We had a lot of land, a lot to cut. This mower was so big it beeped when you backed it up, like a truck, you know? It was a hot day, hot day." A sheen is on Sam's face, as if an August heat oppresses him this moment. "I was mowing and it was so hot I just wanted to finish. The little dog used to ride in my lap on the mower, but it was too hot and I couldn't stand it, you know, the extra weight and heat on my lap. So he was down on the ground and yipping to get up with me, but I left him there and just kept mowing trying to finish in a hurry. I remember the mower beeping because I was backing up, and the next thing my mother is out there screaming. I'd run over the little dog, cut its back legs off. 'There'll be no more dogs in this house ever,' my mother said. That's what she said."

Big Sam sits in his wheelchair with tears running from his eyes and sweat beading on his face and neck. "*No more dogs in this house,*" he whispers. He caresses Hannah's face and she raises herself to him by putting her front paws in his lap. "I'm sorry, girl," he says. He's not talking to Hannah, but I let her answer by licking his salty face again and again.

Just recently I've begun to think Hannah is starting to respond differently to patients' moods and emotions, especially tears. She noses in more gently when someone's upset, seems less fixated on rooting out treats and her kisses are less playful, more nurturing— more like a mother's on one of her pups. Is this attributing too much awareness to a dog? Perhaps. This is a learning process for us both. But here she is with Big Sam, literally kissing the tears off his face, like an absolution.

How often regret is the subject at the nursing home. And not regret over profound life decisions, but over a thoughtlessness, a carelessness, even an accident, no more than lint or a loose thread in the fabric of a life, brushed off more or less easily at the time. It's Herman's regret over his wife sitting out on their porch all dressed up and waiting. It's Big Sam's regret over backing up the tractor mower. I listen to the residents and it's amazing how quickly my own regretted moments come to mind in full color. I know this much: regret is the emotion I most *don't* want to have when my parents are gone. I don't want to blame myself for not being there enough, and I don't want to be ashamed of myself for being critical or impatient. I don't want to miss moments to let them reminisce or speak their fears, because I am afraid that like Herman, like Big Sam, I won't be able to forgive myself. I am already troubled by the times I've fallen short. It has nothing to do with payback, nothing to do with how perfectly they were or were not there for me. This is about my own standard, what I will and won't be able to live with. At the same time, I know there are limitations to my power. I cannot protect them from loneliness, fear, suffering. I can only try to be an emotional anti-inflammatory for the pain of old age and a passionate advocate when one is needed.

And then there's this: I'm lucky. My parents aren't trying to cash in on my effort. In fact, they'll hardly accept help at all, which causes a whole different set of problems. There are parents like my friend Debra's, whose mother rehearses complaints about Debra and her brother like a symphony conductor. When multiple tests, most of which were probably unnecessary, failed to prove her mother's personal conviction that she has cancer, her mother began telling friends that she has "an inoperable condition," and that her children won't take care of her. "My doctors write in my chart that my children are spoiled and selfish," she told Debra recently. What a balancing act we all have to negotiate, to figure out where are the legitimate boundaries between our own lives, those of our parents and those of our children.

Spring is arriving without a megaphone, just whispered announcements. Red buds ripening on the maples. Mourning doves nesting in the Colorado spruces. On the fences outlining fields, bluebirds, and the notes of their distinctive song. Isolated clumps of grass are starting to green here and there alongside the muddy trails, yet it still feels like that nethertime that could be March, could be November.

The flesh of the land is still undressed, all its crevices and rises visible especially where the forest is oldest. No leafy thickets obscure the gorge that holds the little river known as Harker's Run if you're above it, up on the Rhinehart trail. I'll see it come, though. I'll see the greening start at the ground and creep upward toward the canopy even as tender stalks that will sing themselves into wildflower day by day overtake the dead brown leaf carpet. Honeysuckle and saplings will put on pale green chiffon not nearly dark or dense enough to shade the trails and I'll see it, and feel the earth heal itself, and that's what will keep me headed into what's next. I train my dog, I create another book, my children seek my counsel. They likely ignore it, of course, but are kind enough to leave me some illusions.

From either a bed or a wheelchair in the nursing home, there isn't this sense of advancement or change. The windows are set too high for the residents to see more than the sky. For a few weeks, perhaps, a window will open and spring's washed and softened air will reach them. But the air conditioning will go on, at the same temperature as the heat is now, and each day will look and feel like the one before. Of course the mind starts rewinding and replaying regret. Memories are what the residents have, often all they have, with no way to wipe clean whatever tarnishes those memories and make them shine enough to light the rest of the way. *Let me be a polishing cloth!*

The last of March. Buds have fattened on the lilacs, and new wings are beginning to separate on forsythia like nascent yellow butterflies. There's been no ice on the river for a couple of weeks; Hannah's swims don't leave her looking like an oversized paintbrush, each bristle tipped with frosty white. And yesterday a first swarm of gnats thickened the field where Hannah and Betty played tug of war after we emerged from the woods. The air is so soft today, the afternoon so buttery light and warm that it's hard to go into the nursing home. There, like a perverse miracle, the weather is perfectly consistent: seasonless gray, too hot.

"There's someone I'd like you to see," says Carla. She finds Hannah and me in the reception area just after we arrive, which probably isn't difficult thanks to the hoots of laughter from Connie as Hannah does an accidental somersault while chasing the fleece ball.

"A new resident, terribly depressed," Carla says. "She really misses her dog. She's been crying a lot, and I told her you came with Hannah."

"No problem. Who and where?"

"E-2, first bed. Her name is Button."

"Button as in . . . on clothing?"

"That's it."

When I peek into Button's room, keeping Hannah behind me, she doesn't *seem* depressed. Her face shines into a smile when she sees me, but when her eyes, a cornflower blue nearly the shade of my mother's, reach Hannah, she erupts in delight. "Oh bring it in, bring it in," she says. "Oh, I miss my dog so much. I don't miss that asshole husband of mine, not one bit, but I can't bear it here without my Precious."

Button is lying on her bed, the head of which is raised. I guess her to be in her sixties, which will turn out to be accurate. Her straight, steel-gray hair is cut short with bangs swept away from a side part. Regular features around those cornflower eyes that disappear into crinkles of good cheer when she smiles, which is readily and often. The button-like dimples on her cheeks deepen then, too. It's easy to imagine how she was named. There's an alertness, a presence about her that's somewhat rare here except in new residents, before they're absorbed by the giant sponge of stultifying boredom. She's wearing a sleeveless gown that looks like the housedresses both my grandmothers used to wear. Against the wall is an electric wheelchair of the "scooter" type, next to a fairly large television on a stand. A chest has a few personal items on it, and I'm guessing the drawers are stuffed with what she's been able to salvage of her possessions. Hannah noses the bed and Button immediately caresses her ears, the familiar hand motion of a dog lover. I give Button a handful of treats, and she and Hannah are off and running.

Metaphorically running, of course. Button, it turns out, can't walk due to advanced arthritis. She tells me about her thirty-two-year marriage to Rodney, the second for each of them, and how she raised his three children along with the three of her own six still at home. Then came arthritis, seizures, two strokes; Button became increasingly disabled over a couple of years until she was chair and bed bound.

On Christmas Eve, three months ago, Rodney was staring into the fireplace, quieter than even his usual taciturn self.

"You okay? Anything wrong?" she asked. Button tells me she thought he might be worrying about *her*; she had a cough.

"I'm sitting here thinking I just don't want to be married no more," he replied. "Just want to see what's out there, taste the world."

Button snorts as she tells it, but tears rise and quiver in her eyes. "Yeah, that's rich. A sixty-seven-year-old man with a defibrillator stuck right in his ribby old chest, he just wants to go out and taste the world. It ain't the world he wants to be tasting if you get my drift."

So Button found herself with no place to go, no one to reciprocate years of caregiving, and worse, no one who still needed her. None of the nine children have room for her. She says it with slight defensiveness, shoulders squared and chin high, primed for an argument though I've said nothing, as if she knows I'd think one could or should take her in. She hasn't the money to hire someone to be with her round the clock, and although it's almost unthinkable to me, she'll probably spend the remainder of her life confined to a half room shared with a succession of strangers. "I regret every hour I gave that man," she says. "Shoulda stuck to dogs."

She tells me how she got her beloved Precious. A teacup poodle all of four pounds, she says, demonstrating how the dog can sit in her two cupped palms, Rodney brought the pup to her when an acquaintance was trying to find it a new home. Which was shortly before Rodney said he didn't want to be married anymore.

"He knew. He knew how I love dogs, and he knew I couldn't turn it down. That wasn't nothing but guilt. But Precious, he takes a running leap into my lap and he gets up on my shoulder—he still don't weigh but four pounds—and we share my dinner. We share everything. Until I had to come here. I told Rodney, somehow I'm coming back to get my dog. I *got* to have my dog."

Hannah licks Button's hand, the one she just used to catch tears midway on their roll to her chin. Button leans over and looks intently into Hannah's eyes, using a thumb to caress each brow as she cradles Hannah's head in her hands. "You understand, don't you girl? I've got to have my Precious. *You* understand." The light in the room is an unlit twilight gray. The snapshots of Button's grandchildren, the china figurines and plastic daffodils have receded and it seems Hannah's and Button's faces, nose to nose as they are between Button's wrists, is the entire tenderness of the world, our oldest and best story.

Yesterday, in Harker's Run, I saw a mallard pair, the brilliant green head of the male iridescent in the dappled light of the small river. They swam together slowly, obviously a nesting couple. Hannah galloped across the rocky shallows and plunged in the depths, intending to swim over to greet them. The ducks winged off in opposite directions until the male did a squawking U-turn and flew to be with the female. His wings had bright blue patches. I thought about Herman, Mary, Button and the others bereft without their mates and living with regrets for company because there's nothing new growing, nothing that requires their care, their touch, their nurturing, their love. Even now, with the children grown, when I come home I am needed. Hannah does her joy dance at the sight of me, and neither how tired I am nor the weather make any difference: three hundred sixty-five days a year, she gets fed and walked and trained and caressed. Goldfish will rise to a meal; ivy, ficus, philodendra, peace lilies will be misted. I am connected to life as it extends itself, through and beyond me.

Although it's just the second week of April, the May apples, those little green beach umbrellas for elves, have gone from their small, collapsed state to fully open in a matter of days instead of weeks. There are sections of the forest floor so densely carpeted with white rue anemone in full flower that it seems the trail can only be an aisle to a wedding. Lavender, blue, white and even yellow dogtooth violets tumble over each other's edges, not at all shy this year. I've been dazzled by a patch of hepatica boldly, luminously purple-pink as dawn. Time has put on running shoes out in the world beyond the nursing home, the world in which a "golden view" can be something more than either a naïve or ironic concept. The creative activity of participating in, nurturing, protecting new growth—whether it be the forest, a person, a new manuscript, or a dog like my Hannah or Button's Precious—is, at the bone of life, exactly what keeps me engaged and invested. It's also what's most missing for the residents here. I see it every time Hannah eats from one of their outstretched palms.

5. We All Fall Down

"Can you open your mouth, Peter? Take a bite, just try it."

Peter is sitting in a chair next to his bed, not wired to an alarm right now because Helen's there to see he doesn't wander. But he keeps trying to get up, which means he bumps the tray table with his dinner on which there are no fewer than four separate liquids: milk, tomato juice, apple juice, and water. "I feel like I have to open them all, which is such a waste," Helen says. "But I'm afraid if I don't open them, *they'll* think I'm not trying hard enough." She means the staff. I don't mention that they'll pay no attention to whether containers are open or still sealed when they throw them away, because I'm not sure it would be comforting to her. She's not, after all, here to feed him all three meals, only two.

Helen brushes Peter's lips with an eighth of a grilled cheese sandwich. She'll work for the next forty-five minutes and get exactly that much down him. He's in a double room, with no roommate at the moment, an accident for which Helen is deeply grateful because roommates have televisions and visitors and she cannot hear at all over background noise. There's a pine tree outside and I've made far too much of the lovely view, searching for positives in the bleakness. She's been hesitant to decorate, to bring in his own things, fearing that it will make Peter think she's given up on bringing him home. She doesn't want him to feel his being here is permanent.

"I don't want that," Peter mumbles.

"What? What did you say?" Helen asks eagerly. He's not been talking at all, so she jumps on whatever he says. Only she can't hear him because of her own deafness compounded by Peter mumbling into his own chest where his chin continually rests these days.

He ignores her. Or it's more that he's not tuned in now, and doesn't even know she's speaking.

"How about a french fry? Will you try a french fry?"

"I don't want that," he repeats, ineffectively batting at her hand. She has no idea what he's said, but it wouldn't matter if she did. She's as determined to feed him as he is uninterested, a perfect show-down of will and lack of it.

"If you don't eat, you won't get strong enough to come home. Just try. Are your bottom teeth in?"

"Are you ready to go home yet?" Peter says. "I am. Let's go."

Helen misunderstands the first part and doesn't hear the second at all. "Well, I'd rather be here with you. I thought we could talk."

On the floor at Peter's feet, Hannah heaves a deep sigh, as if she's taken it all in and despairs.

Watching Helen struggle to feed Peter puts my parents in the fore-front of my mind. Mom's refrain has, of late, been "I'm just not interested in food," and it's become everybody's focus, as if merely ingesting enough—or the right—magic food will insure against an-other fall, the broken hip we all fear. When Hannah and I get home from Golden View, I make the second call of the day to them.

"I made her a good breakfast," Dad says, "and she ate it. She ate it all. I've got a lamb shank cooking for dinner right now. Have you ever made one? I smothered it with vegetables. So she'll have a good dinner. She's just sleeping now."

"Is she sleeping Dad, or lying on the garage floor?"

He knows exactly what I'm referring to but deflects it. "She's sleeping," he says. "In her own bed."

"You sound like you could use a bit of sleep yourself." His voice is raspy with exhaustion.

"She's up a lot in the night," he says, and the sideways admission might as well accuse me directly: *and you're not here to help*. He wouldn't say or think that under any conditions. I manage that all by myself. Outside the window of my study, twilight is rising off the ground, but I've not turned on any lights. At first I was twisting the phone cord over my head repeatedly, pacing as I talked, but now I'm in my desk chair with my head resting against the computer screen. Hannah nuzzles around my waist, then pokes her nose up between my chin and the monitor to lick my face. I wonder, does it make sense to anyone else how this dog puts herself between me and despair? I move to the floor so I can hug her. Knowing what's coming, she sits between my legs so we're chest to chest, my arms around her. She gives me a quick kiss and then slides her chin onto my shoulder. Sometimes a therapy dog does her best work with her own handler.

I take the comfort of her in. Then, I get up and head to the kitchen where Hannah erupts in rapture as I dish out her evening meal.

Over a period of months, I've felt as if Peter and Helen were giving me a close-up view of my parents' days in a series of parallel events, as both Peter and my mother were falling with heart-stopping frequency. On days when I've wanted to forget Mom and Dad's dilemma because there wasn't a thing I could do but worry, Peter and Helen's proximity have kept my eyes open. For them, these months culminated in Peter's living in the nursing home, even while my parents are holding on by their teeth and will.

I remember Helen's call just as we were finishing dinner one night. "Lynne, can you come over? Peter's fallen again. I need help to get him up." Alan and I dropped our forks and sprinted across the adjacent yards to let ourselves in, as we'd come to regularly since Peter had been growing increasingly confused, increasingly off-balance, prone to wandering and to falls that left him on the driveway or floor, often with a head injury. Is it Alzheimer's disease or the already-diagnosed Parkinson's? Another mini-stroke? A string of doctors, even neurologists have tumbled off opinions like beads falling from a broken string, all landing in a scattered disorganized jumble of uselessness.

Meanwhile, life was very, very hard. Peter, once about my own five feet four inches, seemed to shrink each month, especially as he's so bent beneath the hump on his back that he sees only the ground ahead of him. He'd always been the one to walk their dog, but Helen had to take that over too. Dawn's a sedate and leashed old girl now, but even she could fly Peter like a kite if she took a mind to chase a squirrel. More important, Helen was sure Peter would get lost, even here, in this close-knit neighborhood where they've lived a quarter century in the house they've surrounded with daffodils, an enormous vegetable garden in the one really sunny spot, a Bradford pear tree planted when Peter's mother died.

He hallucinates. The fall I'm recalling now, for example, happened when he sat in a chair that wasn't there. The week before, he'd fixed himself an ice cream cone in the middle of the night. Not so bad, except he was naked at the time, and the ice cream was a scoop of Crisco on a piece of wheat bread. Helen was afraid to go to sleep.

Alan hauled Peter to his feet while I moved a chair into place behind him. Peter passed Alan an imaginary plate of cookies. "Let me call Timothy," I said. "Please. Or you do it. You have to have help. There are decisions to be made and this is too much for anyone."

"He's on vacation now. I don't want to spoil his time. I'm all right." A wisp of white hair had strayed out of the barrette on one side, and Helen brushed it off her forehead. The pin curls she put in the previous night were still there, and a dab of pink lipstick, but she was melting in fatigue. Has she lost weight too? Maybe. She scarcely clears my shoulder now. But, like my Dad, she's kept her health and mobility, and slowly taken over the running of their household and their lives.

Helen and Peter have two sons, the elder in a group home for the developmentally disabled, and the younger, Timothy, an architect in Florida. Like my sister and I, neither is a realistic source of ongoing physical help. Of course, there's not a lot of money. Retired teachers don't have huge pensions, and Helen's afraid to spend what there is anyway. "I'll need it more later," she always says. "Things aren't likely to get better, you know."

I'd asked her many times about calling Timothy. There was always a reason she wouldn't.

It made me crazy. As crazy as the calls *I* don't get.

"I didn't tell you yesterday because I didn't want to spoil your weekend," Dad said on the phone recently. "I wasn't dishonest; she *was* lying down."

"On the garage floor, Dad? With the life squad on the way?"

Mom's legs had, the story went, given out entirely as he tried to help her into the car to take her, ironically enough, to her physical therapy appointment.

My mother's gait bears an uncanny resemblance to a baby's: wide-stanced, tottering, a gait that is a constant sign language for "I'm just about to pitch over." Her doctor has ordered physical therapy to strengthen legs that don't want to work anymore. Mom scorns canes and walkers. "Those are for old people," she says.

Dad had sounded a bit out of breath when I called but immediately denied anything was wrong. I'd asked for Mom; he said she was lying down. So much for a strict construction of the truth. The next day I got the real story. The life squad had helped Dad get her up and said maybe she'd had a TIA (mini-stroke). They wanted to take her to the hospital, but Mom and Dad refused. On her last trip to the emergency room, Mom lay on a gurney in a hallway for five hours before she was even examined. Now she's willing to go to the emergency room if she's already dead, but other than that, no thank you.

Peter's move to Golden View was set in motion by, predictably, another fall. Alan and I had heard the sirens after hiking with Hannah, as we were pulling out from the parking lot at the trailhead, but we didn't give them a second thought beyond the reflexive sympathy they evoke. But the ambulance was already parked in Peter and Helen's yard when we rounded the curve of the road to our house, Hannah between our shoulders, panting and still sopped from her swim.

Another sprint through the yards. Peter had fallen, we hadn't been home when she called us, so Helen called the life squad. More though: he was hallucinating and didn't know her. She'd been up all night with him. He was incontinent, she couldn't keep him in bed, he was conducting an imaginary meeting of old students. Exhaustion seeped from her pores, which compounded her own confusion when the life squad members told her that the hospital might not admit him. Incontinence isn't an admissible illness, they explained, and one never knew how hallucinations would be handled. "Maybe just a tranquilizer shot and send him on home," one EMT said. "It happens." It would, of course, then be Helen's job to get him there; ambulances don't run two ways.

From Helen's kitchen, I called Peter's doctor at home almost begging him to call the hospital and admit Peter directly rather than risk the on-call doctor's assessment. "She can't go on. Give her son a chance to get here." He agreed, though not enthusiastically.

My contemporaries who have already been through this will recognize my request to the doctor as an accidental stroke of genius.

A person on Social Security may be admitted to a nursing home for up to ninety days and it may be paid for *if* he or she is sent there directly from a hospital stay of at least three days. My call to the doctor had insured the first night.

Another day, another fall.

"I can't walk but I've got a wheelchair now," Mom said, her voice on the phone deceptively strong; each time I see her in person, I'm shocked again by her fragility. "Dad rented it from the pharmacy." This time, apparently, a neighbor had been able to help Dad get her up.

"Mom, you *need* to see a doctor." I'd tracked down the name, address and number of an urgent care center near them that is staffed by emergency room doctors. "You won't have to wait. I've talked to them. Have you got pen and paper? Take this down." Mom's doctor was out of town for three days. It's a cosmic rule, apparently; the elderly only fall after hours or on holidays.

"They'll be there," I'd told the emergency facility by phone, relieved that Mom could see a doctor right away, that I'd actually been able to *do* something that would help. "They'll be over shortly. Please take good care of them."

I should have known better. "We'll wait for our own doctor to come back," they insisted while I argued that if she'd had even a small stroke, as the EMT had suggested last time, speed of treatment was imperative. "It's all right; we've got this wheelchair now."

Any long distance caregiver will recognize the dilemma. But I'm learning that even caregivers in the same household can't be there every second, prevent every fall. Her every fall, though, is my own.

Just as I would were someone to summon me, Timothy got on a plane to help Helen as soon as I called him, which was from the hospital lobby while Helen sat by Peter's side in the emergency room. I'd not doubted for a minute that he would. He spent the days (he needed three, remember) of his father's hospitalization running around looking at continuing care options while the doctor cooperated by running tests—discovering only anemia—on Peter. With Timothy, we learned the Catch-22 of the Social Security paid nursing home stay. The patient must be "making progress," showing active improvement as a result of therapy. If he's not, then the stay becomes the family's financial responsibility. For most people, it doesn't take long for that to deplete their savings. Either home care is arranged or, for those like Peter whose spouse can no longer manage, once the money is gone, it's Medicaid time. Timothy had hoped to get the full ninety days possible under Social Security while he helped Helen make necessary large purchases before she had to "spend down" the rest of their assets by paying out-of-pocket for nursing home care. In a perfect world, of course, Peter would have improved. It didn't happen that way. He's in a regular care room now, and Helen's footing the bill.

Her eyes red-rimmed, face ashy with worry, she says, "I'm so afraid he doesn't understand, that he'll think I've thrown him out, you know. But at least I don't have to worry about him falling."

I do nothing *but* worry about my mother falling. And my father.

6. Power

Button lies on top of her bed again, nightgown-clad. The television is on *Days of Our Lives*, but she appears sincerely delighted to see Hannah and strokes my dog's ears with a practiced, loving hand while Hannah noses a combined greeting and quick check for errant food. Button kisses Hannah's nose, and Hannah reciprocates so earnestly and so thoroughly that I have to grab a hand towel from the linen cart in the corridor, dampen one end at the sink, and give it to Button to sponge and dry herself. I'm still working on the canvas bag of equipment I carry with me on these visits. Week by week, I'm figuring out what I need: a couple of soft fleece balls, a tennis ball, various treats, a pen and notepad to leave notes for residents or staff. I jot a mental reminder to add a clean hand towel that I can offer when Hannah's been too exuberantly affectionate.

Like so many of the residents, Button doesn't turn the TV off while I'm here. After asking permission, I sit in her electric wheelchair, the only chair in the room, toward the end of the bed where her bare feet rest. They are swollen and bluish. Her hands amaze me all over again, though. Oval nails, longish and shaped to perfection, the kind of hands I'd more expect on a college girl. A capable college girl, like my daughter, who attends to how she looks.

"Have you seen Precious?" I'm referring to the teacup poodle she had to leave with Rodney, her soon-to-be-ex husband.

"Rodney brought him down and I got to have him here for an afternoon." Her eyes fill.

"Oh, so you saw Rodney, too?"

"No way. I told him not to come in here. I had him bring Precious to my daughter's house and then she brung him here."

"Too hard to see Rodney?"

"I still love him to death," she says. Her tears continue, but her face is not crying. It is almost as if she's learned to ignore them and simply carry on a conversation without being diverted into crying. The mechanical hysterics of a sitcom laugh track explode from the TV. It feels terribly inappropriate to the moment and bothers me, but Button doesn't appear to notice.

"Maybe things might still work out?"

Button scoffs at the thought, energized by remembering her own anger. "No way. Not after what he done, the prick, 'scuse my language. I couldn't never trust him."

"You mean the other woman?"

"That and he blackmailed me."

"Blackmail?"

"He wouldn't sign the papers for me to get the Medicaid, about the money and all. That's the only way I had a place to go, if I could get Medicaid and be in a nursing home. I got to have somebody with me all the time. I can't walk, you know, and I can't get to the bathroom or whatever. Where could I be but a nursing home? He wouldn't sign the Medicaid papers till I signed divorce papers. It's blackmail, that's all. And I had to say I didn't want nothing of his."

"Aren't you entitled to something, after thirty-two years?" I say. My eyebrows must look like McDonald's arches; I feel the incredulity in my face and hear it in my voice. Surely this can't be the right story.

"Oh I suppose I am," she says. "But he don't want me to have it, and I had to have a place to go. The lawyer like to had a fit. But when I go to court, my daughter'll take me to it, and she'll love this, when the judge asks me if I agree to this divorce, I'm gonna say, 'No Sir, I don't agree, but he blackmailed me and I had to sign.' Maybe the judge will make it right, then." Legally, of course, any money Button had would go to pay Golden View anyway, but she seems unaware of this.

I'm thinking of Liz when I say, "You must feel like all of a sudden you have no control over what happens to you."

"It's worse than not being able to walk or drive and having to have somebody with you every hour," she says, nodding. "I trusted him." Button fumbles for a tissue on her bedside table. Hannah is restless— the room is hot and cramped—but I don't want to interrupt Button, so I pour ice water from Button's pitcher into my cupped palm and

Hannah laps it greedily. Another handful and another, while Button dabs each eye alternately, back and forth. A second mental note to myself: add a small plastic water bowl for the equipment bag. And a comfort toy for Hannah, one she'll be content to lie down and chew patiently when a patient who started out talking to *her* moves on into talking to *me*. I realize as I plan how much of my thinking has to do with problem-solving, with having the control and resources to bring about change.

But I'm soon reminded of the larger scale, the one more like that with which the residents cope. A cold front moves in, betraying April back into February. A fierce hailstorm pounds the earth just hours after I leave the nursing home. Wildflowers, blooming trees, tulips, daffodils: all are bent, encased in ice. So much tender, vulnerable life slammed into the ground, injured beyond healing.

The storm is violent and dangerous enough to cancel our hike. The electricity is out and I call my parents from an unlightable gloom in my study. Mom's been back on her feet lately, they've been encouraged, but I still check on them daily.

"Well, Mom fell again," Dad says right away. "She was just standing up, right at the counter, and all of a sudden she hit the floor. I saw her head bounce and I thought, oh no, this is it. But she's fine. I don't see how we got so lucky, but she's just got a big bump on her head."

"But Dad, the fall. What made her fall? Was it . . . ?"

"Her legs just went, she said. She was right at the counter, so you'd think she could have held on, but she said she didn't have time," he interrupts. "I couldn't get to her in time." His tone is remorseful, a skim of defensiveness forming at the edges.

"Oh Dad, I'm sure I wouldn't have caught her either," I say, not believing for a minute that it's true, my own guilt that he's dealing with this alone tracking down my cheeks. I wipe my face with the back of the hand not occupied with holding the phone, that tenuous and invisible connection.

The Golden View is a quadrangle, four wings built around an open central courtyard where bright tulips, hyacinth and daffodils spill color. There's been another weather change, and we're back to spectacular spring, the air a palpable caress, anything indoors seeming wasteful. The sunlight on dogwood and white birch glistens like clarified butter. But when Hannah and I sign in, we check the court- yard and find it as empty as if the whole suggestion of renewal has taken the bypass, leaving this place stuck in a boondock winter. The residents who aren't bedfast are parked in the hallways and com- mon areas, mostly just staring into middle space. No one is outside, although wide glass doors are made to accommodate wheelchairs, and there are benches, tables and chairs artfully placed among the plantings and trees. Instead, a magic marker board in the common area for B wing keeps them informed: "The weather is sunny and warm. The season is spring."

The door to the courtyard is ten feet from the resident parked closest to it. She happens to be a woman of about seventy, I'd guess. Elfin and alert-looking, she's in a baggy pink dress. Her nails and lips are painted hot pink. She grabs my sleeve as Hannah and I pass, but it's not the dog she wants.

"Did you see a loose man around?"

"No I can't say I did. Is he cute? I'll go find him if he's cute."

"Nah. Don't do that. Then you'd keep him."

"Darn right," I say. She erupts in bells of laughter.

But not everyone is able to use humor to pull out the stinger of powerlessness. In another wing, I'm immediately taken back to thinking about how little control the residents seem to have over their own lives, and how it's exactly that control to which Mom and Dad cling, tenacious as barnacles. As I pass through, a ragged woman is seated at a dining table banging on it relentlessly. "Cof- fee," she chants. "I want coffee." It's about three in the afternoon; a cup of coffee doesn't seem unreasonable. The other residents, stashed in various corners, are immersed in their separate, closed worlds and are not roused. The staff, three or four of whom are perhaps fifteen feet away at the nurse's station, completely ignore her. She perks up as I approach and says something, but I can't make it out.

"Did you want to see the dog?" I ask hopefully.

The woman, whose hair appears to have been combed in a wind tunnel and who wears a battered blue print dress with a sweater so old that it's completely devoid of both color and shape, stops chanting and stares at me. Encouraged by what I think is interest, I

repeat, "Do you want to play with the dog? I can bring her to you."
I never bring Hannah directly to a patient without an invitation.

"I don't want no damn dog. I want coffee." The chant resumes.
"Coffee. Coffee." Now a fist drumming the table accompanies it.

"Shut up, Ruthie," Big Sam says politely. It's one of the few times
I've heard one resident talk to another.

Ruth ignores him and keeps right on going. One of the aides calls
out, exasperated, "Later, Ruth. I'll get you coffee later."

This literal off-putting is fairly common; I've seen it before. Rose
is an articulate widow in her early seventies whose son lives in town,
but whose daughter-in-law is the one who provides attention and
personal touches like the little white lights strung around her own
artwork, plants, and personal momentos in Rose's crammed half of
the room. She was in the hallway last week trying to talk to a nurse.

"May I have a snack?" she said politely. The nurse didn't appear
to hear. "May I please have a snack?" Again, no response, though it
seemed impossible the nurse didn't hear. Rather, she bustled away,
back turned. Rose shrugged and asked me to take her back to her
room. I have trouble imagining the sheer frustration of being an
adult and having to ask, almost beg, for a snack at a time that's not
scheduled. The loss of power over one's own time, appetites, simple
decisions like *I think I'll have a cup of coffee*—now, not later—is
unnerving when I try it on for size.

At the same time, for sure, I'm aware of many attentive and caring
gestures on the part of the staff. Even in Rose's case, when she and I
got back to her room, she pushed the buzzer to ask for help getting
from her wheelchair to the upholstered easy chair she'd salvaged
from her own home. Perhaps fifteen minutes later, an aide came.
A girl of about twenty, sweet-faced and smiling, ashy blond hair
arranged in cornrows, blue eyes crinkled in perpetual good humor.
She hoisted and arranged Rose, positioning her catheter bag.

Rose tried again. "May I please have a snack?"

The aide looked around the room. Sure enough, there were two
Lorna Doone cookies left in a package, half a can of Mountain Dew.
"How would this be?" she asked.

Rose looked dubious, but I could tell her innate good breeding
made her reluctant to seem a pest. "That'll be okay, I guess," she

said, the subtext being *that's not what I want, please ask me if I'd rather have something else.*

The aide, however, doesn't hear that or perhaps she's learned it's best not to, though she often strikes me as the one I'd most like to have attend to my mother. Or me. "All righty then, wonderful," she said cheerily, unwrapping the cookies and positioning the straw in the can. "Just call me if you need anything else." I cannot imagine my Army officer father somewhere he cannot bang out an order he fully expects to be obeyed. I cannot imagine my mother, who would hint around as Rose did, humiliated with cheerful caring.

The whole issue of how much control we can claim and preserve grows increasingly important as we age. For the past several months, Barb has been struggling with hip pain that makes our dog hikes excruciating. This is a woman accustomed to at least two hours of exercise a day, often considerably more. She and I do weight lifting, land and water aerobics together. On top of that and our walks, Barb teaches an exercise class two times a week at the senior citizens center, cuts and chops all the fuel for their wood stove. She's slender and extremely fit, extremely limber, her dancer's body still evident at sixty-three.

Of late, though, she's increasingly debilitated. No clear diagnosis yet, just pain in one hip that increases by the week through test after test, specialist after specialist. Yesterday was the first day this week she even tried to hike, and she had to stop repeatedly as spasms overtook her. Barb is not a woman to ever give in, especially not to pain. For her to forego our dog walks, and forego them when the forest is jumping with magical color and life after having been out there in freezing rain and every miserable condition winter has to offer, she has to feel it's way beyond simply unwise. Her depression is palpable. There's almost a sense of outrage in us both. *This isn't right*, we think. If I can't fix it myself, then I *have* to be able to *make* somebody fix it. When she tried to walk with me yesterday and couldn't, she said, "I can actually understand how people get to the point where they want to end it. I've never understood that before. You start asking yourself, 'How much of this can I bear? How much is worth bearing?' " Coming from a woman with as much heart and sheer strength as Barb, the questions are unprecedented and frightening. And what if she were to decide she wanted to end it and, like Clare, lacked even that power?

I'm still stuck on this issue—power—as Hannah and I swing in to see Button, stretched out on top of her hospital bed, a metal trapeze hanging above so she can pull herself up and shift position. Her bare feet, ankles and legs have the same bluish pallor again but are more swollen, her toenails now in serious need of cutting. She can't reach them herself, of course. When my sister Jan and I visit our Mom, we have toenail cutting sessions for her and gauge by the length how overdue we are in coming.

As always, the television is tuned to a soap opera, *General Hospital* this time. Button wears a sleeveless lightweight gown, white, V-necked; a wide stream of mid-afternoon sun pours through the closed window and overheats the room.

As we enter, Button smiles at Hannah's wagging approach, but starts to cry an instant later. "Rodney moved somewhere, nobody knows where and he took my Precious. I don't know where my dog is. I'd be all right if I could just have my little dog. I've got to get my dog back. It's in the divorce papers. He has to give me my dog."

She reaches for Hannah who makes a quick decision and jumps up on Button's bed. "Oh let her stay!" Button cries as I start to snap my fingers and order her off. Left to her own devices, Hannah circles her tail a few times and then stretches out alongside Button with her head on Button's stomach. I sit in the wheelchair by her bed and we talk about Precious and Rodney for a quiet half hour. Button strokes Hannah's ears while I hold her free hand. Sometimes she talks to Hannah, sometimes to me. Often when she's crying, she addresses Hannah and the dog raises her head to make eye contact. It all works just like a movie of animal-assisted therapy at its best. Until . . .

Until, that is, Hannah happens to catch sight of a Mylar balloon in the far corner of Button's room. Who knows if it's the smug grin of the cat pictured on it or the fact that the balloon is bobbing about slightly in the warm air that causes Hannah to spring up to save the world from this menace? She barks, leaps the length of the mattress, and flings herself toward the ceiling where the balloon lurks a good seven feet off the floor. I swear she misses it only by inches. She gives several warning barks as she backs up to get a better running start for the next attack, this one to be launched from the floor.

The opportunity for empathy and discussion evaporates. The only benefit is that now Button is having herself a thigh-slapping belly laugh while I am, of course, dying of embarrassment as my magnificent therapy dog demonstrates the excellence of her obedience training and my control. In front of an audience, of course. If I wait another minute, I'm sure Hannah will jump up on Button's roommate's bed and use it as a new tarmac—she's now eyeing its convenient proximity to the enemy—so I drag her out for a hallway lecture, promising to see Button again after the balloon has escaped or died.

I make my way down the hall toward the exit, detouring to Mary's room where I find her asleep on her bed, and then to Clare and Edwina's room for a quick hello while the Fire Engine Lady is quiet. I begin to squeeze Hannah into the narrow space between the two beds so both women can see her. Hannah apparently decides she has now developed a whole new approach thanks to her experience with Button, and startles me by leaping up onto Edwina's bed where she immediately sniffs out a stash of Oreos Edwina has secreted under the covers. I wrestle the package from a bitterly disappointed dog, hastily shove it back under the quilt, and drag Hannah off the bed, while beginning my now-memorized apology script.

"Oh that ain't nothing. I ain't afraid. I'm used to Lucy," Edwina eagerly interrupts to remind me.

"Yes, I know you are."

"She ain't right in the head. Came in here and said these was her cookies," she says, pulling the package back out from underneath the covers and waving it over her head triumphantly. "I told her she was a goddamn liar trying to be a goddamn thief."

Now any dog person will have immediately realized that my having stuffed the cookies back under Edwina's quilt didn't fool Hannah for a minute. All I really accomplished was to let her know that it was off limits. Edwina has now brought the package right back into play, and, unfortunately, I mean play in the most literal sense of the word. When a highly desired object is waved around in front of Hannah's highly sensitive nose and the highly desired object involves chocolate, Hannah is rendered stone deaf to all commands, especially *off*, and *leave it*. And, also unfortunately, when she goes deaf, she does not go mute. While Edwina is waving the package of Oreos she has successfully wrestled from the clutches of the wannabe thief Lucy, my dog is quivering with glee, yipping at each flourish of the package because it signals that Edwina is about to throw the whole magnificent booty to her in the world's greatest new game. I know what Hannah's thinking. She's thinking that tennis balls are now passé. She's thinking that Edwina is her new best friend.

For the second time in ten minutes, I have completely, utterly, and totally lost control. I am feeling sick. This scene is about to give a whole new meaning to "tossing one's cookies."

"Uh, Edwina, I'm afraid Hannah thinks you're going to give her those cookies. Would you mind putting them back under the covers?"

"Just tell her to ask nice. She ain't no goddamn thief. If she was a goddamn thief, I'd have to whip her butt, too. I'll give her a cookie."

Oh no. "Well, that's very nice of you. Maybe if you just give her one little piece of one, and then put them away." Of course, I'm wanting to shout PUT THOSE DAMN COOKIES AWAY! but am still clear-headed enough to realize the staff might frown on my shouting at a patient, especially while my (big) dog is simultaneously barking at her. After all, Edwina weighs less than Hannah and is bedfast, even though she did credibly threaten to whip Hannah's butt. This probably wouldn't make us look good. Might get us fired.

"Hannah, sit." Hannah and I are both panting at this point.

Hannah instantly plops. She's hot for an Oreo; having previously raided these at home, she already knows she loves them. Two more quick barks in case Edwina hasn't noticed that it's time to pay up.

"Make her ask nice, now," Edwina says. "I don't like no goddamn rude ones like that goddamn liar Lucy."

Oh Lord. Hannah is literally salivating on the floor. "Hannah, shake hands." Hannah complies. Another reminder bark.

"Edwina, this is how she asks nicely."

"Make her sit up and beg."

"I haven't taught her to do that. She can bark for you, though."

"Make her beg right."

"Um, Edwina, she doesn't know how to do that. I can't teach her that right here now."

"Ain't she smart?"

Now I'm torn. Do I try telling her that my nice smart Lab has a learning disability just to see if we can bypass this mess, or do I try to explain it rationally? Hannah is leaking out a little whine, which means she's warming up to explode into more barking. I can't take it any more. I'm ashamed to say I sell Hannah out on the spot. But I whisper so as not to hurt her feelings.

"Well, you know, not so much."

"That's a problem, she don't know how to do it right. Me, I do things right. I solve my own problems. See, Lucy, she tried to say these was her cookies, she's a goddamn liar, so I keep them under my covers now. If she tries to touch them I'll whip her goddamn ass." With that, Edwina abruptly stuffs the cookies back under her covers. Hannah blinks and shakes her head, disbelieving this treachery. I'm extremely proud of the instinct and reflex combination that makes me shoot a restraining hand onto her collar; Hannah is definitely not above a stealth leap onto Edwina's bed in a search and rescue operation for those Oreos. Then Edwina would have a new goddamn thief whose ass she'd have to whip.

Now Edwina's finished with us. She's solved another problem herself; her cookies are safe from liars and thieves. She's already spinning herself into a nap on a web of mumbling about whose butt she's going to beat next.

Clare has, in her quiet way, immensely enjoyed the show we've put on. I catch the grin she tries to hide as she pretends to be absorbed in a PBS showing of *Carmen*.

Of course, Edwina has a point. Being *able* to solve one's own problems is the core of control. I'd want it, too. I *do* want it, too, and doubtless, it's why my parents fight my attempt to be "helpful." *They* want it, too. I need to keep reminding myself.

Clare and Edwina probably have just about equal measures of actual ability to solve their own problems, but are polar opposites in their reactions to dependency. Edwina denies and fights it, while Clare has an aura of acceptance that gives me pause. I move to her bedside in the oven of their half-room, liberally trailing consolation kibble to Hannah, hoping I can learn how she's achieved it.

Today, Clare's just had her shower (it happens on a room rotation, twice a week) and her washed white hair is still damp, freshly rebraided to snake from behind to lie on her chest. "Where do you find your patience?" I ask. "Do you have some faith that keeps you going or is it a matter of digging down and grabbing hold?"

She had to think quite a while. "I do have some faith," she gets out in her labored way. "But that's not why I'm patient. It's just . . . I have no other choice. Sometimes I get very jittery inside, waiting for them to do something. But what can I do?"

It's a rhetorical question of course. She's saying she's relinquished power, control, and autonomy with simple, quiet dignity because there's absolutely no alternative that isn't plain exhausting in its fruitlessness. Could I do this? Honestly? Or would I take Edwina's route, a feisty shadow boxer against my infirmity, fooling no one except myself?

I move on, shifting the subject just enough. "Has your daughter been in to see you lately?" I'm expecting a yes, but I should know better.

"No . . . she's just terribly busy. She runs an art store, and they're fixing it up."

I make a murmur of sympathy and Clare says, "I know I make excuses for her." Suddenly I wonder if my mother makes excuses for me. Where she's concerned, how often I make that trip is about the only thing I'm in control of.

7. Whatever It Takes

So two weeks later, I don't make it to the nursing home at all because I'm with my parents. In non-crisis times, I do my best to get here every other month, alternating with my sister, so that, ideally, one of us goes monthly, but even when we're successful, it's not enough. There's no family near them; I'm the closest at a two-day drive or an expensive air trip with a layover. It's never easy to suspend my professional and personal lives while I exist a few days, maybe a week, whatever time I can steal to be with them in their world. Believers in the power of relentless nagging, Jan and I regularly beg them to relocate near one of us, but it's been perfectly ineffective so far.

From the kitchen table in their home on the North Carolina coast, I watch a snowy egret fishing for breakfast in the spartina of the inland waterway. The house my father built on the land of his dreams is all light-filled, expanses of windows over the marsh and water at its back. A pestilence of wild onions has taken over the pine straw of the front yard, the conditions for their proliferation having been precisely perfect after the hurricane last fall. I've spent hours during this visit tugging them out by the roots, four herbicides having proved completely useless over the past couple of months. With what abandon life proliferates, and then how tenacious it is. Tiny white onion bulbs are everywhere as I spade square foot by foot to loosen their tentacles before I'm forced to my hands and knees to yank them up. They surrender with a ripping sound, clinging one to another to another under the surface of the earth where they have burgeoned like barnacles on underwater rocks.

Life holds on to life. Yesterday I took Mom to her doctor. Marcia Fretwell seems the ideal geriatric specialist: respectful of Mom's autonomy, a good listener who focuses on quality of life and natural antidotes whenever possible. We discussed changes in Mom's diabetes medication, the prognosis of the giant cell arteritis that has limited the sight of one eye, the idiopathic autoimmune disorder that keeps her perpetually on steroids, the osteoporosis, the tremors in her head, the weakness in her legs that brings about sudden dangerous collapses. Sometimes, when I look sidelong and just observe, I see the physical diminishments. She's under five feet now, hunchbacked, snail-slow with a walker, which she resists using anyway, as dogged as a prizefighter. "Those are for old people," she reminds me again disdainfully. A wheelchair has been an off and on necessity following the falls that, I can't help thinking, the walker might have prevented.

Dad, too. The arthritis in his ankles and feet is not better and, to my eye, might be worse. The labor of maintaining their large property seems greater and greater in proportion to his ability to do it, although he insists it's what he wants. Just as he insists he wants to and can take care of Mom. When he gets up from sitting, he helps himself with whatever stable surface is available, and his steps are rusty, halting. I see how he's adapted emotionally, adopting a mellow, "Ah, if not today, then maybe I'll get to it tomorrow" stance, one to send my perfection-focused and sidelined mother right past *Go* to land on *Insanity* without collecting two hundred dollars. Sometimes I get a slantwise view, though, that there's turmoil roiling inside. His youngest brother, the one who moved to California forty years ago, is still in the neverland between living and dying. *What's the point of this suffering?* Dad asked me twice as we sat over coffee this morning. I know he's thinking about Mom, himself, and the future. So am I.

Today, Dad—a retired Army colonel—is up at the Camp Lejune base hospital to see a dermatologist for the new eczema that has his fingers and feet bleeding from hairline cracks in the roughened skin. Last week it was another doctor, the one who's watching his elevated liver enzymes. On small fronts that surround them, my parents fight to hold their ground. A check goes out to have the plumbing fixed, then one to have the roof repaired, another to have someone come cut down the hurricane-deadened giant pines, eyes always on the balance of what remains. I remember Liz, back at the nursing home, without the money to share a pizza, whatever the reason. Here, the car quits and has to be replaced. Mom checks the stock quotes each morning to bemoan what they didn't buy or sell in time while Dad counts out their pills, lining them up on the kitchen table like miniature soldiers forming a battle line. It's a privileged existence, to be sure, yet they fight the same war as those with much more money and much less. They want their lives.

Before Dad left for the base, though, he made a rare reference to eventual defeat. We'd been talking about their friend who'd been in a nursing home for several weeks, but who's come home now and seems to be doing well. John had returned to the facility to visit, bringing chocolate for the staff and the men with whom he'd shared a room. One of the roommates hadn't recognized him, though John had only been discharged a week earlier.

"John says that poor guy's just shelved until he dies." Dad observed, "It's a morgue for the living." An index finger jabbed at me. "I won't let that happen to Mom," he said emphatically. "And don't *you* ever let that happen to me." He was backlit, sky and waterway light pouring through the glass, his features faded, but his sparse hair outlined strand by strand.

"I have no intention of letting that happen, Pop," I replied. What I meant was that I'd have him with me, or I'd come here, whatever; *somehow* he'd be cared for by his family. That, however, wasn't what he meant.

"You know," he said, "last year there was a big thing around here. A man and his wife both had terminal cancer and one day he took a gun and shot her and then used it on himself. A lot of people said that was terrible, but to me, you know, it was courage. I've had a talk with the doctor up at the base. I told him that if there's no hope for me, I want him to give me what I need to end it, and he says, sure, he sees my point and he agrees with it, but no way will he put his license to practice on the line." He pinned me like a butterfly with his eyes then. "The government has no business telling me I have to live. Shoot me if you have to. You'd show Hannah that mercy. Whatever it takes. If there's no hope, I want to die. I do not want to be a pain in the ass to people."

The opening was a plum begging to be picked. "In that case, Pop, you should have died fifty years ago." Laughter erupted. But then I forced myself back because we need to talk about this and it's hard enough just to begin, which he'd made himself do. Dad's philosophy is a little to the right of Attila the Hun, and I am his pinko liberal dismay, but we meet at the border: insistent on autonomy, and *control* of our own living and, by extrapolation I now see, our own dying.

"Whenever the time comes will be too soon, but when it does, if you are suffering and ask for help to die, I'll find a way. I'd hope for the same for me from either of my children." This from me, a woman who volunteers with her dog in a nursing home and who believes they can be improved enormously; this is what came to my lips without hesitation or reservation.

"Thank you," he said, and labored to rise from the table to leave for his doctor appointment. "I got eleven grapefruits on sale yesterday, the red ones," he said, as though it were a sequitur. "You know, I spoon them out and freeze 'em for when they're out of season. I'm laying in a good supply."

"I'm not counting you out yet, Pop."

"Good," he said, his step heavy, slow on the way down the hall. I went outside to get after the wild onions, still alive and rooted in place, like us.

8. Working (in) the System

Back home, southwestern Ohio leapt from spring into mid-summer while I was gone. Even though May has scarcely begun, the maples still launching pods on the breeze, the trees have gone to full leaf in a week of unseasonable 80-degree heat. Even the dogwood, whose blossoms were all palms up to the sun like hope, have leafed out, gone to green. On the trails, the vegetation that had only accomplished half of its rise to treetop level when I left has shot the rest of the way up; the uppermost canopy has filled in, shading and cooling the path. Really the only remaining evidence of spring is the late wildflowers. The white violets are having a banner year and the phlox, a soft lavender mauve, literally line the trail, a fairyland scene. The heads of the sweet Cecily are miniature Queen Anne's lace, and golden Alexander is a bright high yellow. Wild geraniums have started to bloom alongside the clear blue of Jacob's ladder and the startling white perfection of star of Bethlehem. There's a great deal of both in the riparian areas, along with the periwinkle blooms of waterleaf. Except for the violets and star of Bethlehem, all of these flower a couple of feet off the ground. Hiking the riverside trail, especially, feels like being in a green tunnel, it's that close and dense. The flesh and bones of the land, readily visible in winter, are completely obscured by these layers and layers of clothing. Honeysuckle is blooming, its distinctive, rich perfume riding the smallest breeze, but it's an unwanted interloper in these woods. Non-native to the area, its choking proliferation crowds out the good hardwood saplings.

Last week, Hannah startled up a groundhog and chased the poor, slow creature back and forth within the same circle near the up-stream footbridge over Harker's Run. She only wanted to play. Her tail swung in great arcs of friendship while the terrorized groundhog desperately tried to escape.

Betty sniffed out the situation, recognized that there was no fun to be had, and retreated to Barb, whose hip is enough better that she could hike today. But, of course, Hannah wouldn't. She'd gone stone deaf while Barb and I got hoarse shouting at her to *leave it.* So much for training. The groundhog finally turned and stood, probably planning its death fight. Hannah apparently thought she'd finally convinced it to play with her and tried to kiss its face. It attacked, which made Hannah back up in confusion, and the groundhog fled after biting Hannah under her eye.

This was closely followed by Hannah (on a different trail, one that edges the outside of a stable and several corrals for a brief distance) slipping under a fence to bound over and make nice with the grazing horses. A bay mare and an appaloosa in particular didn't want a new best friend and gave chase with apparent intent to kill, since the appaloosa reared twice and the general effect was that of a furious stampede. Hannah stood a moment, dumbstruck by this ungracious welcome, then wheeled and frantically quartered back and forth to elude them and escape. Too panicked to remember where she'd come under the fence, she ran up and down it with the horses in hot snorting pursuit until she found the sweet spot. This was accompanied, of course, by humans screaming instructions, blowing Hannah's whistle, idiotically demonstrating how to get under the fence, and generally adding to total mayhem.

These incidents made me think of an e-mail recently forwarded to me, one of dozens I get each week. This one suggested that one should "Love as if you've never been hurt." Hannah will bound in tomorrow just as ready to love any creature she happens upon as she was yesterday, when she might have learned caution instead.

What do the staff think about working at the nursing home, I wonder. What are their thoughts about their aged parents? About themselves, and what will happen when they're, say, in their eighties? Do they—or don't they—dare to empathize, to care, to get attached, to help residents preserve autonomy and control?

How do the ones who care for these old people keep on loving in the face of assured loss? Mary has an answer: most of them don't. She's been on top of her bed, the hand-knit afghan over her, the past couple of times I've come. If she's been awake, she's said she didn't feel well enough for a visit, and I've moved on quickly. Today I swing

by her room for a quick check expecting the same and am surprised
to find her up in her wheelchair, stylishly and tastefully dressed in an
aqua sweater coordinating with a silk print blouse and pearls, hair
as orderly as undisturbed new snow. The second surprise is that Liz
is with her, and Mary is crying. I enter the open doorway in response
to Liz's gesture and put my hand on Mary's shoulder.

"I just want to be treated like a human being," she says.

"Of course you do. Who are you upset with?" I say, squatting
on my haunches since Liz is in Mary's easy chair. (She's one of the
very few who *have* such a chair.) I'd recognized her half-room as
homey the first time I came here, when Mary was the first resident
to whom Carla introduced me, but experience has made me even
more aware how rare that aesthetic is here. But Mary never expects
to go home; she's come to terms with calling the facility her home,
and perhaps that unusual lack of denial is a factor in how the room
is personalized and arranged to maximize privacy.

"Oh these people, the ones that work here," she says. "This morning I put my (call) light on and waited. I had to go to the bathroom.
One of those snot-nosed aides came in and turned the call light off—
she thought I didn't see her because she stayed behind the (room
divider) curtain—and then she just went out. I put the call light on
and waited forty-five minutes for someone to come take me to the
bathroom. What if something had been really wrong? But how'd you
like to wait forty-five minutes if you had to go to the bathroom?"

As Mary speaks, Liz nods in confirmation. Mary doesn't notice.
Still crying, she says, "I was just so furious. I'm tired of it. I *pay*
to be here. I *pay*. It didn't used to be like this. I've been here nine
years. It used to be different. They had nurses, and they were in
white uniforms, and they stayed." She dabbed at her eyes. "Now
new aides come and they don't get any training, and they only get
paid six and a quarter an hour. So they leave in two weeks."

Liz says, "Well, I don't know how it used to be, but it's true the
help doesn't stay. Especially the aides. There aren't many nurses,
except on the skilled wing." I knew what she was referring to only
because after a couple of perplexed months, I finally figured out that
the "skilled wing" didn't refer to the patient's skill level, but to the
nursing skill required for their care.

Mary is paying no attention to Liz now. She's hot on the subject and wants to spill it. "One time I had my TV on. I can't hear, you know, and I couldn't sleep that night so I had my TV turned up so I could hear it. Dodie had been calling out all night, don't you know, so I sure wasn't keeping *her* awake. Well, one of the aides, Jill her name was, she came in and said, 'I've taken about all of this I can take,' and she just switched off my TV. I *pay* to live here. I wasn't bothering anybody but Jill, and she just didn't like my show."

Liz murmurs assent. "They do get annoyed a lot," she says.

"And they don't even keep people clean," Mary says, speeding on through the verbal intersection. "Dodie gets sores because they don't change her enough. But when you need to go to the bathroom, they don't come. What is she supposed to do?" Fresh tears start. I immediately think of my dad when Mary says, "They shouldn't force people to stay alive. A lot of us don't want to. That's all I hang on to now, that this'll be over soon and I'll be gone."

All negative perception of the staff honestly surprises me. Liz evidently reads my face. "It's not that there aren't some nice ones," she says. "There are. The ones who talk to us like human beings are probably the same ones who have gone out of their way to talk to *you*, too."

"David's really nice," Mary interrupts. "He'll sit on the bed and talk to me when he has time. But, don't you know, he's an agency nurse. He doesn't really work for this facility. There's this one nurse that comes in on Sunday nights, and I just dread to see her. She makes everybody miserable."

As she speaks, I'm thinking of David and how, yes, Liz's right, he does go out of his way to speak to me. He also gets down and plays with Hannah every time, warmly, for maybe thirty or forty-five seconds before he's up, washing his hands, and back to work. For every five staff members I see, there's probably only one that has actually seemed aware of my presence or interacted. (The staff almost universally responds to *Hannah* with smiles, caresses, questions as to her age, breed and gender, but I am distinguishing that from any awareness of me other than as Hannah's handler.) Carla has been my main impression of the staff, I realize. Maybe she's not entirely representative. And then I think of my Dad, backlit by sun on water, a military haircut even now when there's hardly hair to cut, an index finger impaling me on each word to make them stick forever. *"Don't you let that happen to me."*

As I started to observe staff more closely, it became clear to me that this would become the most difficult chapter to write and, then, to read. It is sad, and it's tempting to omit, but that doesn't seem either right or respectful. Too many are trying too hard with too little—too little education, too little training, too little support, too little pay, and an environment that is, after all, no more nurturing to them than to the residents—not to include the issue in honest depth. This is not about bad people who don't care, and if it's cast that way, it masks the real needs.

One thing is clear to me. Some of the rules here get in the way, exacerbating the sense of powerlessness and, therefore, hopelessness. When I saw Liz again a week later, rather than her long hair being peppery gray for three or four inches out from the roots until it reached a demarcation zone, all of it was a richly shining deep brunette, left free to its own curly will. I immediately said, "Liz, your hair looks *gorgeous.*"

"Thanks. A friend brought me a do-it yourself kit because my kids won't let me have any money to have the hairdresser do it. It got me in trouble though."

"Why?"

"I'm not allowed to color my hair here."

"Why not?"

"I have no idea. I mean, I did it in my own bathroom. Nobody was around, I cleaned it all up, I didn't leave chemicals out for anybody to pick up accidentally. Just . . . rules."

I admit this makes no sense to me. Surely there could be a way to accommodate a woman coloring her hair and feeling good about how she looks. This is a fairly minimal degree of control over one's self, after all. My mother would give up almost anything before she'd give up having her hair done weekly and getting a fresh permanent four times a year. Dad drives her, and he and the hairdresser help her to and from the car.

Both Liz and Mary are on the residents' Executive Council. "Could you bring this up at Council?" I ask. "Shoot, I'd come in and help you color it if that's the issue."

Liz snorts, exactly as Mary has before on the subject of the council.

"That's a complete waste. *Nothing* ever changes no matter what we suggest. I've already told them I won't run again."

The next week, I pursue the Executive Council with Carla: What is it? What power do the residents have through it?

The power of suggestion, mainly, I glean. Carla says that the Executive Council is an elected committee, representing the Residents Council, of which all members are technically residents. Meetings of both are led by the social worker. In the Executive Council, the representatives may make suggestions, pass on complaints, propose activities, and "work on" facility projects such as the on-going effort to raise enough money to buy and maintain a van.

But here's what Mary and Liz agree happens. They meet. Liz raises the issue of the Fire Engine Lady, her constant wailing and chanting, how inescapable it is and how many of the people on her wing are bothered. (They keep her more drugged during the day, Liz says in an aside, because they don't want visitors or her family to hear how bad it really gets. "Then, at night, they park her in the common area and let 'er rip.")

"We've had no complaints about that," the social worker will say.

"Oh come on," Liz will say. "There's nothing *but* complaints about it."

"We'll have to look into it," the social worker will answer.

Nothing happens. The Fire Engine Lady, with her repertoire of repetitive noise-making techniques including high-pitched yodeling, chants, and simple wailing is left in the wing she's assigned to (as opposed to grouping the Alzheimer patients together, for example). During the day, she's often parked in the lounge, which means no one can watch the big screen television or do an activity or carry on a conversation. The sound is penetrating and, indeed, as Liz has put it, inescapable. Nobody from Administration gets back to the Executive Council with an explanation. It's as if there had, indeed, been no complaint.

I ask Carla about it. She listens, nods, and says nothing. She seems perfectly happy to respond to questions of fact, but each time I've brought up an issue that could be construed as a criticism, she's had no comment at all.

And another thing to puzzle: the nursing home literature says that there are scheduled "case conferences" during which the care plan for individual residents is discussed. Patients and families are encouraged to attend and participate in these team meetings, which are led by the social worker. After I became aware of this—because I snagged a copy of all literature given to patients and families— when Liz says she has no idea what's to happen when she's eventually discharged, I ask what they'd said in her case conference. She's never attended one, she says.

"Have you asked to?"

"No, I guess not."

"Have you been told when it's happening?"

"No."

I have a secret image of myself that involves a painted face and colorful feathers, hopping in a great circle to drums and war cries as my faithful dog prances in perfect rhythm around the fire with me. Recognizing that I am dancing on the edge of being seen as a troublemaker, I suggest that she might want to tell the social worker that she wants to attend the next one.

Still mystified about this, because if there's a single resident at the center who'd be capable of participating and taking active responsibility in her own treatment plan, it would be Liz, I go through the skilled wing hallway toward the common area where Big Sam is always parked. Once he's flipping Hannah's fleece ball into the air for her to catch on the fly, I ask him how his plans to "get out of here" are proceeding.

He stops flipping the ball and shrugs. "Dunno. Waitin' for the doctor to let me out." Another inmate-like statement, only needing the substitution of *warden* for *doctor*.

"When might that be?"

"He says I got to be able to take care of myself."

"Hmmm. What exactly does that mean? What will you have to be able to do that you can't do now?"

Another shrug. Yet Big Sam is not mentally incompetent. Not even a little mentally disabled. Why isn't he exactly clear on what constitutes "taking care of myself" and engaged in putting together the jigsaw of independence and dependency that would give him back his life?

"Well, do you talk about it in your case conferences?"

"What's that?"

"The meeting, you know, when everyone discusses how to help you help yourself. Making plans."

"Never heard of that," he says. But he doesn't seem upset and he doesn't pursue it.

Later, after I'm the one who tosses the fleece ball and narrowly misses a resident's head to Big Sam's chortling delight, I ask him how the Residents Council works.

He's totally perplexed. "What's that?" He insists he has no idea.

He still might not know about the Residents Council, but if he had family actively involved, he'd surely know about the case conference. Here's what I've concluded: the patients who have family here almost daily, as a few do, overwhelmingly get the best care because the family members do it. Yes, the food is brought in on a tray, but it's the family members like Helen who coax it down patients like Peter. It's family members who go get an aide when a diaper needs changing, family who bring in books, video tapes, pictures, wall decorations, plants, see that clothing is attractive, clean, in good repair. They provide company, attention, all the intimate kindnesses and touch. And they bring in grandchildren, great-grandchildren, an occasional cat or dog. One middle-aged son brings in a caged blue budgie. Most of all, they bring in the perspective of the outside world, where there's more hope, more power. It's they who stir things up at a case conference if any stirring gets done. Helen has already asked when Peter's first conference is. She'll perhaps be too inclined to accept what she's told, but she'll ruminate on it, ask Timothy or me, and hesitantly go back to request a change.

As she did with medication, for example. Peter's been difficult or impossible to rouse. Helen often spends the whole afternoon sitting next to him as he sleeps in a chair after sleeping through the lunch Helen struggled to feed him. Finally, she's asked that he be taken off the medication to control hallucinations. Maybe that will help, maybe not. But if Helen hadn't asked for the change, I do know there wouldn't be one. Few patients are less trouble than sleeping ones. When I see in close-up focus how much direct care Helen provides, I realize all over again the implication of not being there to do it for my parents.

Two weeks later, all through a darkly cool June afternoon punctuated with thunderstorms, I sit at a card table with Liz and three staff members of the Activity Department. We are sorting inexpensive beads, which they're stringing into necklaces and bracelets to sell at tomorrow's yard sale. The yard sale, a giant mélange of baked goods, donated used clothing, a scattering of lamps, old radios, gadgets, and craft items made by the residents, is to raise money to repair a rickety fourteen passenger van which has just been given to the Center. The van will be used by the Activity Department for "field trips." A mall, a park, a movie, the zoo or just uptown for one of the free summer concerts, all have been mentioned as possible destinations.

Judy, the activity director, pulls up a chair and joins the group. I'd guess she's rounded the corner of her mid-forties and headed for fifty, though I can't imagine she'll use any ordinary map. Today she's dressed in beige shorts with a fancy belt, stockings and flats, a heavy gold necklace over the coordinating shirt. Coiffed like a teenager, her bottle-blond hair ponytailed in a black scrunchie and further fancied with spit curls and tousled bangs, she doesn't touch a single bead. I can't quite see what she *is* doing, but what's unusual today is that I see her at all. It was Judy whom I repeatedly called for an appointment about volunteering here, and Judy who never returned my calls. I'd been coming for several months, in fact, before I saw her at all. Nobody knows her schedule; her staff often call her at home if they have a question or problem. Conversely, Carla, the activity coordinator, is always here, always available, always pitching in. It was Carla to whom the receptionist finally referred me when, asked to leave yet another message, I commented that there seemed little point since none of my calls had been returned. It's Carla, too, who's warmly supported my visits and continually directs me to people who'd benefit from contact with Hannah.

Judy doesn't stay long anyway. I ask Megan, a twentyish girl, fresh-faced, thick brown richly curly hair pulled back from her face in a barrette, what exactly Judy does. "What's the difference between the activity director and the activity coordinator?" Her first answer was a shrug. "Well, *Carla* is our boss, even though she always says she's not a boss," she answers. "Judy does . . . paper work, I guess." Julie, sitting next to Megan, rolls her eyes. She's in her mid-thirties, a natural ashy blonde, round-faced, on the heavy side, and has been telling us all repeatedly that her dog nods yes and no in response to questions. She holds up the necklace she's just strung for us to admire. "Well, it's nice if you're . . . uh . . . colorblind," Liz says, but with just enough tease mixed into her honesty that she pulls it off.

"How does working here affect you?" I ask Megan. She's two years out of high school, I've learned, and "activities" is the third job she's had here, the first having been in the dish room and the second as an aide.

"At first it was really hard when patients—I mean residents, we're supposed to call them residents—died. When Luther died, oh, I cried and cried and I couldn't stop. After so many, though, you sort of dull to it. You have to."

A couple of weeks later, I spoke with David, the nurse about whom Liz and Mary spoke so highly. It's a Sunday, an afternoon so oppressive that the air between storms is a sticky quilt smothering us, and he's in the last eight hours of two sixteen-hour shifts, which is how he spends every other weekend. I'm propped up against the nursing station panting because I've just prevented Hannah from killing a resident. Michelle, the outgoing nineteen-year-old aide with beaded blond cornrows and blue eyes that crinkle and disappear into her enormous smile, had been heaving Hannah's fleece ball down the length of an open hallway just to see Hannah turn on the afterburners as she sped to fetch it. A resident came out of her room without her walker; Hannah assumed she wanted to play and went bounding up to greet her. Based on the rate of tail wag, I anticipated the French kiss approach and raced to throw a body block on Hannah. So while I'm gasping, I'm also crediting myself with saving the old woman's life. I'm also deciding I'd best not stay too long, because Hannah's not herself. The heat may be bothering her, but the Fire Engine Lady is ten feet away, too, and her steady, high-pitched wail is unsettling. *Where . . . is . . . my . . . mother?* She keens it over and over today, like a relentless howling wind that pierces your mind, and I'm thinking it's why Hannah is off center, using too much of her strength, scrambling in an antsy way after the ball. Normally, here, she knows to put herself in low gear. I give the hand and voice command, "Down. Stay," and try to settle her on the cool tile floor so I can still my heart and talk to David, who found the rescue hilarious.

He looks seventeen, has one year of vocational school practical nursing education, and he's in charge of L wing for the entire weekend. (An RN is on duty, supervising the facility, but stationed on another wing.) Without using Megan's name, I tell him what she said and ask how that matches with his experience.

"Maybe I just see things a little differently because I'm a guy," he says, sorting medications into labeled trays as he speaks. He's slender, perhaps five eleven in height, with short light brown hair that curls in this steamy heat. A navy T-shirt spells out Golden View Nursing Center in white letters across his chest, but, really, white pants and shoes are the only indicator that he's on the staff at all.

"I'm twenty-three years old and I've been through a number of full codes, when I've done CPR and all the emergency procedures on people that I knew were already dead. But you have to, you know, unless there's a DNR (Do Not Resuscitate order). And then I go out and drink with my friends. It really doesn't bother me that much. I mean, I think about it, but I can still go out with my friends and have a good time. But death and the people are different. I just keep them separate."

"So you don't feel that dealing with so many deaths desensitizes you?"

"Well, I don't plan to stay in nursing forever. I think the older nurses, yes, they probably do get desensitized, but I don't think it's death that does it. I think it's years of being understaffed and underpaid. They get angry. I'm not going to let that happen to me."

So for David, it's not all the death that dulls him the way it does Megan. It's overwork and underpay. I wonder if it isn't also the relentless sadness of the residents' lives that the staff can't bear. Perhaps Connie is an exception, perhaps a few others like Big Sam whose mellow temperaments make them more adaptable, but overall, the residents here are not happy. And I notice that often the staff almost never can allow the sorrow to be expressed. They'll try distraction, or insist someone "cheer up!" or "smile!" For whatever the reason, though, the conclusion seems to be that yes, working here dulls you.

Does it have to be this way because most residents are old, all are either sick or disabled, some are dying? No, because there's this: Hannah loves coming to work, and why wouldn't she? She is fussed over, petted, hugged, kissed, played with, fed, by *staff* as well as residents. Of course, both groups want to be more empowered overall, and they should! Yet, look at what one relatively small, essentially free addition to the home accomplishes. Hannah changes the atmosphere of whatever wing she's on while she's there, and everyone wants her back *tomorrow*! She cannot change what is, yet she brings happiness. And she points in the direction of where to find more.

9. Huntin' Home

Hannah's made a career out of getting into trouble lately. Last week as we were driving through this university-centered town, she spotted some students tossing a Frisbee in the historic square mile around Sycamore Street, one on one side of the road, one on another. This isn't unusual here, especially on a day like that, so sweet-aired and light it seemed a sin of ingratitude to be indoors. Playing on a little-trafficked side street lined with trees and old houses converted into student rentals, they'd just wait for the occasional car to pass. Which I did, Hannah in the back seat as usual, her eager head out the window, ears and dewlap jowls flapping in the breeze. A quarter-block later, I slowed for a stop sign.

I didn't even realize it until I heard shouts of raucous laughter: Hannah had pancaked herself out the half-shut car window and galloped down the road into the middle of the Frisbee game. She was leaping into the air trying to snatch it while the students played keepaway with her, all of them enjoying it immensely. I had to park and run up a one-way street to retrieve her, apologies spilling around me like so many dropped coins. They were unnecessary, it turned out; the students begged me to let her keep playing.

Hannah would have been quite happy to. Just as she's perfectly happy to slip out of the yard and go visiting in the neighborhood instead of assisting Alan in his battle against the moles and their lawn-destruction campaign, until one of us misses her and goes in search. Usually, she's romping with an unfortunate ever-tied-up mutt two yards away. She seems, sometimes, to have no sense about staying home, and I worry that her limitless, trusting friendliness could lead to our losing her.

On the other hand, I remind myself of what happened right before Hardy's heart surgery, when Hannah was lost in the woods. Hardy had gone ahead with Betty thinking Hannah was with Barb and me, while we assumed he had both dogs with him. Probably Hannah had gone on one of her deer trail forays in the meantime and since I'd not realized it, I hadn't stopped to whistle for her when the trail split. A hard icy rain pummeled us as we tramped into dusk on human and game trails, while we called ourselves hoarse. I was frantic and tearful, afraid I'd never see Hannah alive again. The woods are enormous, occasionally bisected by a road, surrounded by rural farmland. People abandon dogs, or pick them up without intent to look for the owner, with fair regularity. It was nearly dark when I ran into another dog hiker who'd heard me calling Hannah over and over. "She was out where you're parked waiting for you," Kim said. "Your car door was unlocked so I put her in. I hope that's okay."

Okay? I wanted to kiss her. "They make their way home, you know," she added. "It's a really strong instinct. Dogs know their people and their home."

And *people* know their people and their home. Mom and Dad, for instance, in their house, their dream house that Dad built twenty years ago right on the Intracoastal waterway, where there's always a breeze on their porch and they track the arrival of spring by the yachts that pass on the way back up north, not by wildflowers and mating ducks. The house and yard are too big, too much. On one of my visits about a year ago, Mom was determined to get a new bedspread and curtains for their bedroom. She can't walk in the mall and is adamant that we cannot use one of the free wheelchairs the mall provides: "They're for people who can't walk." Dad did not buy up the entire stubbornness market, I've discovered. Mom holds stock in it too.

"Mom, *you* can't walk." I lost the struggle to keep frustration out of my voice.

"I *can* walk, I just have to go slowly and hold your arm."

But she couldn't. The turtle pace and arm-holding business were good for about twenty-five steps. We tried, she couldn't go on. I did manage to swallow back the *I told you so*, which should qualify me for both a humanitarian award and a direct pass to sainthood. So we made our way back to the car where she sat in the big silver Mercury Dad has babied for a hundred thirty thousand miles, and I went and bought what I thought she'd like, ran it out to the parking lot, where she said she didn't. I ran back into the mall, returned it, bought another bedspread, took it out to be disapproved. Four times I did this, running each time, not wanting her alone in the car. This because she and Dad love their home and won't leave it regardless of its practicality or manageability.

Home. It's a constant theme at the nursing "home," and one to break your heart.

Dodie, for example. Today, while I'm visiting Mary, her roommate appears just outside the door in her wheelchair. She's not been in the room anytime I've visited. Mary told me the staff keeps her out where they can watch her because she's always trying to escape.

She's trying to say something to me, though I've really not known her previously, and I leave Hannah with Mary and go out into the hall. Dodie is so child-sized that I have to sink to my haunches to be able to look at her face. A diabetic, she's sometimes perfectly lucid, Mary has told me, and sometimes makes no sense at all. Either way, there's only one theme to her intelligible sentences and the garbled nonsensical ones: going home. She is obsessed, always trying to slip out, to make her way home by hook or by crook. The staff put an alarm on her at night as they do on Peter, one that sounds if a patient tries to get up. Of course, Dodie's alarm regularly wakes Mary out of her sleep since only three feet and a curtain separate their beds.

Dodie's voice is so quiet I have to lean in to hear her. "Will you take me home?" she says.

"Oh Dodie, I'm so sorry, I can't do that."

"I have to go home. What are you going to do about that?"

Her face says she's in her seventies, but her hair looks almost like a faded blond rather than the grayish white that is the uniform here.

"Dodie, I wish I could help you."

Her eye contact is direct and insistent. "*It's the only home I have,*" she says slowly, distinctly, explaining simple facts to a dimwit. "I have to go home. What are you going to do?" Her implication is unmistakable. No decent human being could or would fail this challenge.

I try again. "I understand how you must feel. You want to go home."

"Will you take me?"

"Dodie, I'm so sorry, I can't do that."

"Why not?"

Finally, when I cannot deter her, I take the coward's way out of this endless loop. Squeezing her hand I say I have to get my dog because Mary must be getting tired of taking care of her. Dodie stares after me, her whole face declaring that yet another person has let her down.

"I don't know where her family is," Mary says. "Her granddaughter comes and does her hair every now and then, but that's all."

Of course this whole episode bothers me deeply. I cannot imagine my mother begging me to take her home. I cannot imagine my father drilling, "What are you going to do?" and my being able to withstand it. Is this why, sometimes, families *don't* come?

Sometimes when residents talk of home they mean an afterlife. They'll refer to their idea of heaven as "going home to be with God." Usually, though, they're talking about the last home they had before the nursing home, the one they never believed they were leaving for the last time. And they still don't believe it. Even Helen still talks about bringing Peter home. She coaxes food into him morsel by crumb, saying, "You've got to get strong enough to come home." When she says it to one of us, Alan and I say things like, "Wouldn't that be wonderful if it could happen." We cannot bear to say, "Helen, that's not going to happen, you know. How can we help you adjust to this crushing and unwanted change?"

Margaret, a resident I just met, one who is wheelchair-bound and often confused even as she manages to sound completely lucid, said it well, if inaccurately. She and her roommate Annette discussed their dogs as they fussed over Hannah. Margaret, her head a mass of tight mousy gray-brown curls, her small nose weighted with thick glasses, said she knew her German shepherd Rex gets confused since Margaret's move to Golden View. "That's what happened the other night," she says to Annette.

Annette, in her nineties but more clear-headed than I on my best days, answers dryly and non-committally, "Oh really."

"Sure. You remember how he jumped on your bed when he was looking for me."

Another "Oh really," from Annette, though the tone is indulgent, not sarcastic.

"Sure. Then he went on out the window again. Middle of the night. You remember."

Then Margaret turned to me with the explanation. "He's confused, don't you know. That's how they do. He don't know where we is. He was huntin' home. It's instinct, huntin' home."

And elegant Annette, in her skirt and matching blouse, her stockings and strands of pearls, just nodded from her wheelchair and confirmed, "Really."

Understandably, Liz, only about fifty, talks a good deal about "when I get out of this place." Today, she's in a pink Harley David-son T-shirt and black sweatpants, and her dark hair is showing a good deal of gray at the roots again. "They sold my house and came with trucks to pick through all my belongings. They took everything and scattered it between them," she reminds me. "Who knows what I'll ever get back when I get out of this place?"

But when I ask what her plans are, she shrugs. "My home is gone. I don't have anything anymore. I don't know. I thought maybe with my daughter . . ."

Becoming part of her daughter's home was always the plan she mentioned. But something's gone quite amiss there. Liz was to spend four or five weeks with her married daughter last month. The trip was arranged, Liz was excited, and it was clear this was to be some sort of trial. But she was back in ten days and there's been no more talk of returning. Her house was sold, her furniture and possessions parceled out amongst relatives; what does "home" mean now? Like so many of the older residents, the nursing home is not home, but there is no other. In my mind, I can hear my father chanting the mantra that's worn grooves into my brain like an old, long-play vinyl record. "I will not leave my home. They can carry me out of here feet first." It's not a wish, the way he says it. It's an order.

Herman is another involuntary exile "huntin' home." Each time I see him, he gives me an elaborate description of his home, "right there on Route 27, the white house that's just past the Shady Nook, a red mailbox out front." It's the house with the porch where his wife sat waiting while he was playing pool and flirting in town, the house in front of which his little dog was killed. It's *home*, and he talks about how the doctor won't let him go yet, as if a doctor could imprison him here. What he needs is home health care, I imagine, and it's expensive and hard to come by. But he owns a home he hasn't had to sell yet. How is the bill at the nursing home being paid, and wouldn't home health care be less expensive?

Theresa, too. I hadn't seen her in months, but there she was, still in her wheelchair, still inexplicably paralyzed, still "waiting."

"You had the MRI, right?" I ask.

Theresa snorts and adjusts her crocheted multicolored lap robe. Her hair is combed today, but it still looks like a worn-out Brillo pad. "Pffft, I had every test God ever thought up. One of 'em said I got MS but then they did another one and that said maybe not." Her skin is a ghostly pale translucence.

"You mean . . . ," and I'm casting about for a reasonable way to rephrase what she's just said, but one eludes me. "But . . ."

Theresa shakes her head. "So I'm waiting."

"For?"

A shrug. "I dunno. Just waiting. To get me some answers so's I get to go home." Which will, she says, have to be with her daughter. The one who has virtually nothing to do with her since Theresa tried to steal her baby. I'd like to be a fly on the wall during *that* discharge planning session.

Big Sam says he's waiting too. What landed him here was a broken hip. I've learned he's seventy-two, not in his late fifties as he looks. But he lived alone, fell and broke his hip. He can't go back to his second floor apartment, he says, because there are stairs to climb to get up into it. Unmarried, none of his family remains living. He can't move to a first floor apartment because he, well, he can't climb stairs to get his stuff out of his second floor apartment. No, he says. There's nobody to help him.

Catch-22. "Or maybe it's Murphy's Law," he says. He's big all over, but his stomach looks like two basketballs stuffed under his shirt, one sagging lower than the other. Sam looks a little like he'd have trouble walking even if he hadn't broken a hip. But he's hardly more disabled than my mother has already been, off and on. She's had a bevy of home health aides sent by the county.

Can't we do better for people? Must they live for years and years in a half-room shared with a stranger, even people whose minds are fine? How many of the people here have just slipped like water through bureaucratic cracks and administrative black holes? What

I know, having worked for government and private agencies, is that there's always some explanation for ridiculous waiting-for-Godot situations like Theresa's. What I equally know, especially seeing it again here, is its profound effect on people, their *feelings*, their *lives*. Without a smart, articulate, spirited, unwilling-to-take-no-for-an-answer family member, one who pushes and pushes and pushes the system, nothing happens. People sit in wheelchairs and wait. Years pass, hospice takes over, they die. Simple, expensive, ridiculous.

In my mind, I'll be that smart, articulate, spirited advocate for my parents if there's no alternative but a nursing home. My sister will cover my back. From seven hundred miles away? Well, I think, surely *then* they'll be willing to move. There's no way they can watch out for each other, not the way I can. Dad has difficulty hearing. Mom's timid, accepting whatever an "authority" says as the direct word of God. (Unless, of course, *I* am the authority, in which case I am dumber than cement.) So this is where my thinking stops, dead-ended into mapless terrain.

I've watched Helen—hearing-impaired, like my father—flounder at dealing with the facility, Peter's doctor, and the doctor's partner, who she finally learned, had doubled Peter's anti-psychotic medication (for dementia symptoms) while his own physician was on vacation, effectively putting Peter in a stupor. It was unexplained to Helen, and inexplicable. Her son tries to help from a thousand miles away but Helen can't understand what he's saying on the phone. Sometimes, she says, it feels like navigating a foreign country with no translator, no lexicon and no friendly natives. There are other patients and patients' families here who could help her, but she doesn't know that, or them.

What a difference it would make if there were a nursing home in which it were possible to make a psychological and physical home. "Home" usually involves the expectation and need of our contribution—be it to people, animals, fish, birds, plants—even as we are likewise nurtured. There are a hundred ways at least half the residents here could help one another if the model were one of community. Could all participate? No. Could enough participate to change the dejected, passively angry mood? I have no doubt about it.

While I was in Mary's room as she translated frustration and fatigue into tears and Liz patted her hand, the Fire Engine Lady started up another wailing chant out in the hallway. Maybe that's what got Dodie going again, begging for a ride.

"*I . . . am . . . going . . . home . . . now*," the siren-voice yowls, over and over and over. "I am going home now."

10. The Eden Effect

During late May and early June, southwestern Ohio might as well have been Southeast Asia. We're in the midst of a monsoon season run amok on the wrong continent. Day after day, torrential rains punctuated by violent thunderstorms raised Harker's Run and Four Mile Creek into muddy floods churning downstream. When the dogs leap in, they travel diagonally, instinctively avoiding too much fight with the current. Last week, Hannah did one of her four-splay-legged leaping belly flops off a bank into a part of the river she's not been in before, deeper and faster than even her usual swim spots run. She was after a hanging branch the river slapped up and down as if an invisible hand were teasing her with it. Immediately, the current licked her up and spit her twenty yards downstream. Now she wasn't opposite the branch at all, but the concrete base of a bridge. She struggled, Barb and I screamed to her. Young and a strong swimmer, she fought her way back, but an older, weaker dog would have, I'm sure, drowned. She recovered immediately; I can't say the same for myself.

The trails are muck again during these weeks. The other result is that all the vegetation, already rich, has become almost tropically lush, encroaching on the trails from each side and overhead. Fire-pink is the only new wildflower, its high scarlet bloom adding to the sense of a tropical garden, humid, loamy-smelling, fertile, prolific life spilling from prolific life. Daisies dot the high grass around the junipers in the successional forest on the high Reinhart trail that circles off from the spring-fed ponds. At Big Pond, the larger of the two, beavers are working on another dam now that one lodge is complete and secure. Blackberry bushes are in sweet porcelain pink bloom and the mating mallards cruise the far end except when Hannah is doing her exuberant belly flops, flying up to ten feet off her favorite bank to disturb the quiet enough that they hide. The pond is a patch of cool peace, a circle of sunlight floating on its surface making the bull's-eye for Hannah's leap. Eden. It nurtures my soul. It would anyone's.

I've become lax about leashing Hannah when we come into the nursing home. Now she greets Connie on her own while I sign us in. She seems to get it, that she needs to stay at heel and stick close. New residents in wheelchairs occasionally pull back, gathering their legs to the side, and I call out that she's safe and friendly as I take hold of her collar to visually reassure them that even if they think I'm a demented liar, I'm a demented liar with a solid physical grip on the dog.

More often, though, Hannah's being unleashed seems to encourage residents to see her as available. A light comes onto a face, a hand drops from its sedentary spot on the lap and hangs down inviting a kiss. Someone will look at me and the look is a question mark, to which I respond rhetorically. "Would you like to see the dog? Her name is Hannah and she's here to be with anyone who'd like a visit." Usually, the resident has been a dog owner, dog lover, and instinctively as well as experientially knows that Hannah is okay to caress. And usually Hannah sniffs and kisses not only the hand but halfway up the arm, the whole back half of her body wagging with the pleasure of being welcomed. There is very little laughter in the home generally, but Hannah makes them laugh.

There's a brief history of animals in this nursing home. A staff member brought in a mixed breed puppy to live there as everybody's permanent dog. A completely wonderful idea that didn't work out, I've been told by a number of staff, because the puppy never calmed down and was "too much," piddling on the floor every time he got excited. Evidently, that was often. This was much more a nuisance to the staff than to the residents who got a kick out of watching the exasperated clean-ups. After that, there were two stray cats. The story on them isn't clear except that they disappeared. A beautiful golden retriever came to visit with a volunteer who plays the piano for sing-alongs, until the dog died a quick cancer death at scarcely five. Occasionally, family members will bring an animal when they come to see a specific patient. Those dogs or cats do not seem to be shared much; I notice residents seem to stay clear and not seek contact when someone's striding down the hall purposefully, animal in arms or on a short leash.

Think of it this way: if a small child approaches with her parent obvious in the background, it seems there's *de facto* permission from both parent and child to squat down and talk to the child. Even a light touch isn't forbidden. Would I initiate the same conversation with a child marching steadily ahead while holding his parent's hand? Only if I'm hankering for some jail time. So it's deliberate, this off-leashing of Hannah, and she seems to understand what she's supposed to make of it. She's learned to approach the residents slowly, tail wagging, waiting for an outreaching hand or voice before she nuzzles up close. (This is in astounding contrast to her style out of the nursing home. On the trails, she bounds up to anything on two or four legs and immediately attempts to greet new and old friends with her trademark kiss.)

Studies suggest that filling nursing homes with live plants, animals, birds and children yield amazing benefits. Believing that loneliness, helplessness and boredom are the principle causes of suffering in nursing homes, William Thomas, MD, has developed the model of encouraging residents to be caregivers as well as receivers in a noninstitutional human habitat (the Eden Alternative) that keeps its members connected with nature and community life (Thomas, W., MD, 1996). Staff and Elders (as they are termed) share power and decision-making; Elders are appropriately autonomous, individually and in "neighborhood" groups. Liz could color her hair green if she liked, and Button could have Precious with her and seek help caring for him as needed. People would not be sitting alone, staring at blank walls and ceaseless television. They might be reading to a child from an attached day-care center, tending plants and pets, sharing poetry, dictating memoirs to a high school student, helping a less mobile resident. Big Sam, Mary, Herman, Theresa, Button: more of the Golden View residents than not have the capacity to participate, to give, to meet needs. My dad is currently one of the male volunteers who literally drive patrols at night in their already exquisitely safe neighborhood. It's not a stretch for me to imagine what men and women of similar temperament and training might take on.

Imagine what Liz could do! How many vegetables and flowers

could she raise? What poetry program might she plan? What library of community and family-donated books might this voracious reader organize given space and "permission." How many children might she tutor? She, and a number of others who have their minds if not their legs, are college graduates. If they'd like to let elementary school children practice reading aloud to them—and they would—why can't they? Couldn't some be paired with at-risk children, as buddies? Button would read to a child or play checkers joyfully. So would Mary. They would be needed again. And they *are* needed. As would be the person who might raise the fish, or see to the cats, feed and even exercise a dog exactly as Big Sam works with Hannah from his wheelchair now, keeping her scrambling.

Does Edenizing work in practice? Apparently it does and very, very well. The Texas Long Term Care Institute at Texas State University-San Marcos has studied the Eden model, which Dr. Thomas first developed in New Berlin, New York.

When I think of a nursing home where there are quiet areas for visiting, reading, a kitchen for capable residents to use themselves; where my hair color is my own business and elders discuss and vote on management issues; where community is actively built; where gardens flourish, indoors and outdoors along with animals and birds, I feel hope. That is nothing short of miraculous when I compare it to life at the Golden View. Anecdotal reports from residents of facilities that are Edenizing suggest that they are what nobody here is: happy, and at home. Do I sound as if I've suddenly climbed on a high horse and launched into preaching mode? The reasons are simple, straightforward, utterly personal. Mom. Dad. Peter. Hardy. Barb. My husband. Myself.

Poet Sydney Lea wrote a line that I love: "What is hope but futility for moments stood on end?" It seems that hope is what's most missing in the nursing home because it is so narrowly defined. Hope has, I think, to do with the ability to affect—even in small ways—what happens to oneself and whatever one cares about. It's the ability to bring about positive change. It's exactly why I'm at the nursing home with Hannah.

The lull of July. No wildflowers to speak of in the woods except a few weedy composites with tiny, high blooms; they, and the other lush ground vegetation, are almost waist high, straining for light because the canopy is so dense. Big Pond is growing algae on its surface, and in spite of pounding thunderstorms that split the heat of the day, the creeks and river are much lower. The ducks are molting; last week Hannah came upon one floating placidly on a deep pool between small rapids in Harker's Run. Her tail beating a joyous arc, duck wings beating a furious, squawking escape six inches airborne, Hannah chased the poor thing a good quarter mile. She, of course, thought it was playing with her. At some point she got the message and trotted back to me, disappointed, but ready for the next surprise.

At Golden View, staff are taking vacations which means that there are more temporary nurses, more times when they're flat short-handed and everyone gets less attention. The residents who do have visits from family members get fewer visits because adult sons and daughters are off on their own vacations or schlepping kids to base-ball practice and swimming lessons. Even I am getting ready to take vacation with my husband. There'll be three weeks when I don't come in. Yet what does this season of overgrown, abundant life mean in the nursing home? There's no garden corn spiking up, no tomatoes reddening in the sun; no one's outside for the chiffon morning cool on her skin. Out-of-school children don't chatter here. July might as well be January, that's the total difference it makes for the residents here. At Mom and Dad's, there are green peppers and cherry toma-toes Dad is thrilled to harvest from containers on their porch, right between the geraniums he wintered over. There's pink sugar water he painstakingly mixes up for his hummingbirds, orchids he babies and repots, homemade soups he prides himself on. And once in a while Mom can stand up long enough to bake her chocolate mint bars.

To implement the Eden Alternative at Golden View would cost comparatively little in terms of the overall cost of operating a nursing home. Most of the money would go toward education and space reallocation. There is no franchising or profit involved, only an evolving alternate *model* of a human and humane environment that transforms the nature of the nursing home experience.

Even patients who cannot actively nurture people, plants, or an-imals benefit from being around them. Today, a nurse stops me to ask if I'd go to another room with Hannah. "His wife and daughter thinks he's depressed."

There's a man of indeterminate age in the bed to which she sends me. Salt-and-pepper-haired, a pale, puffy face with a six o'clock beard, overweight. At first I think he's developmentally disabled, but then I realize he's a stroke victim. One hand is bent at the elbow and lies across his belly, a stuffed dog between his arm and his body. A bleached blond, big-haired woman of perhaps thirty is in the chair next to him. A boy of about six prances restlessly and tries to stand on his head. Hannah, of course, darts in to plaster his upside-down face with kisses. The child screeches and crawls under the bed.

"Can he see the dog?" the woman asks, dragging the child out by an ankle, but indicating by pointing her chin that she means the man in the bed.

"Of course. This is Hannah. She's a year old, but Labs are puppies until they're two." (I still paste this information into conversation just in case Hannah eats a patient's slipper or knocks over a pitcher of water with her table-clearing tail wag.) I lift Hannah's front paws onto the bed. "Would you like to pat her?"

The man seems a bit frightened, but the women croon and encourage him, his wife taking his dead hand and making it bat clumsily but gently at Hannah's head. He gurgles, and his mouth twists toward a smile.

The women crow. "Oh my God, did you hear that? Daddy? You *like* that, don't you?" shrieks the big-haired visitor. Face alight, she turns to me eagerly and says, "Can you stay a little while? That's the first time he's laughed since he had the stroke! He hasn't even laughed at his grandson." I glance over at the older woman. She's crying and nodding as she guides his hand.

11. Interim Report

Alan and Hannah and I spent two weeks traveling in the Canadian Maritimes, visiting Hardy and Barb at their summer home in Nova Scotia. Hannah and Betty, ecstatically reunited, chased down ocean waves and each other, scampering across the craggy, rock-strewn inlets with graceful confidence as the humans picked their way gingerly over ancient stones and boulders. Hannah was a stirring sight the first day she cavorted at the sea; she'd suddenly stop on the beach and raise her head, standing still with eyes at half-mast to sniff her salt-air Canadian heritage with all the concentration and intensity of blood memory.

During the time we were together, the four of us received word of unrelenting rain and subsequent flooding at home. Harker's Run and Four Mile Creek, into which Harker's empties, had overrun their banks by as much as three hundred feet in spots. One of the suspension footbridges had been washed out, ripped from its moorings eleven feet above the riverbed.

We'd thought we could envision what had happened, but when we got home Alan and I realized just how poor our imaginations had been. The trails were buried in silt, the lush undergrowth that had proliferated during weeks of heat and humidity all bent and broken in a uniform direction. Stately old deciduous trees had toppled into the water as the current ate away the banks of the small river. Now they lie like narrow bridges bank to bank, their roots ripped out, upturned, exposed. Tangles of underbrush had caught against trunks and remained there, piles of brown debris to rot. Even a couple of miles upstream, the horsetail grass that grows green all winter, spiking out of the snow unbroken by the worst of our ice storms, was flattened, unable to straighten itself from beneath its silt blanket. The bridge supports had snapped on one side, releasing the strung-together boards to the current. The supports on the other side held, so when the water sank back within its confines, the whole length of bridge was beached on the opposite bank, looking for all the world like a bent and abandoned train track.

By the time we were home, the water had receded within its newly widened and altered banks. Hannah, Alan, and I picked our way along in horrified amazement, our feet sinking in the fine silt as they would on a dry beach. The weather had taken a nosedive and crashed in misery territory where it languished, day after day, in a torpor of heat and humidity. The woods felt like the Amazon rainforest, with dying vegetation hanging out of the lower branches, and swarms of mosquitoes and noisy insects reacting to our repellent as if it were an alluring appetizer.

I felt as if the flooded area of the forest had suffered a stroke. Not a stroke to take its life, like clear-cutting and paving, but a stroke like, perhaps, Herman's. One to leave its victim almost unrecognizable and require long, long rehabilitation to get all the way back and still be never the same. "It's completely natural, Lynne," Barb says over and over now that she, too, has returned and seen it. "It'll all come back. A year from now you won't know it happened anymore. The banks are different, of course, and yes, the lower bridge is gone, but you'll be used to the changes in shape and course by then; the undergrowth will be back, the horsetail grass will be back, and it'll all look as you'll think it should."

That's Barb for you. But I am trying to listen to her, mourn less, and take comfort in the fact that the great grandmother of the forest, the giant, ancient sycamore with the cavernous hole in its trunk like the honey tree in the Winnie the Pooh books, big enough for an adult to climb in and hide—the great grandmother still stood.

I've not been to the nursing home in over three weeks by the time I get back there. Ironically, Herman, the resident to whose condition I'd compared the flood damage, is the one whose condition has most altered while I was gone. I find him alone in a three-bed room in the skilled wing.

The television is blaring, but he's sound asleep when I come in. Carla told me he hasn't had any visitors and is lonely, so I wake him. As his eyes focus, his face lights. "Oh, it's the pretty doggie lady."

"Why, thank you, Herman."

"I mean the pretty doggie," he says, of course.

"So what're you doing all lazy in bed, instead of out pestering people?"

"I took a bad fall. Spent a couple of days in the hospital, and now they've got me in here instead of my regular room."

"Oh no, what happened?"

"I was trying to get my remote control. Somebody put it up on top of the television, and I wanted it. I was on my walker, ya know, doin' real good on it, too, but when I reached up for that remote control, one leg just give out and I went down hard."

"Did somebody see you fall?"

"No, I just lay there callin' help, help, help for maybe fifteen minutes until finally Big Sam heard me, and he called a nurse. Three of 'em come in and hauled me on the bed, but then they called the doctor and I had to go to the hospital. I'm all bruised up, but I didn't break nothing." He shows me his left arm, which is, indeed, a mess of nasty bruises. "My whole body is like this under my clothes."

I see immediately how much ground he's lost. He's flat on his back with his knees bent over a pillow and his feet in bootie-like cold socks. A bedpan is nearby.

"Oh Herman, I'm so sorry. What a terrible time it must have been for you."

"Oh yeah, it's been two weeks in hell. Thought I was dying when I was on that floor calling for help and nobody come. I'm thinkin' maybe it's time anyway, you know? I don't want to hurt like this."

"I'm pretty sure it will get better," I say, knowing I probably shouldn't. On the other hand, bruising does get better. But something has settled in the hollows under his eyes, and the pupils look dull, occluded.

And how changed the goals are now. Instead of huntin' home, he's in a twilight zone of deciding whether he wants to set his heart on getting himself back onto a walker or, like Mary, on the good deliverance of death.

And Herman's not the only one. When I came in, Connie wasn't in her usual spot near the main entrance. Even Hannah had nosed around looking for her while I signed in and rooted in her bag for the special collar and tag she wears while working. As I made my rounds, I kept circling back to check her spot, thinking someone had taken her to the bathroom, but it stayed empty. Finally I ran into Carla. "Connie's in bed," she explained.

So after spending time with Herman and fetching the picture of his wife off the wall in his old room so he can open his eyes to her every morning again, I find out where Connie's room is, and Hannah and I head there.

At least the ritual hasn't changed entirely. "Come here, my baby, come here, my baby, baby, baby," she croons and Hannah bounds to the bed where Connie is sitting up but wearing a blue print hospital gown. Her long black hair is in its usual bun, and her fat cheeks look painted pink, though she wears not a speck of makeup. Fairskinned, dark sparkle-eyed, Connie could fit a description of Snow White except for her size, which is huge. Now her feet are stuck out, uncovered, immensely swollen and bluish, though I have no idea if this is unusual since I've always seen her dressed.

"Connie, I missed you out front! We don't know how to sign in without you there. Are you all right?"

Connie, however, is undeterred from Hannah who, of course, remembers that Connie always feeds her. Right away her front paws are up on Connie's bed and Connie's closed-claw fist is waving toward Hannah's bag of treats as she chants her "my baby, my baby, my baby" mantra.

"Why are you in bed, Connie? Are you sick?"

Hannah is washing Connie's hand and arm, and intermittently nosing under her arm. I wedge kibble into Connie's hand. As usual, as many drop out as remain in place. Hannah vacuums up the ones on the white sheets immediately then sets to work on the ones hidden in Connie's rigid fingers.

"My legs is hurtin'," she answers.

"Do you know why?"

"I think my bones is just, like, dissolving or somethin'."

"Has your doctor explained what's wrong?"

"I got . . . ," she struggles for the words and has to pronounce them several times before I can repeat them approximately, even though I am getting better at understanding her distorted speech. "Friedrich's ataxia."

"Goodness, Connie. I've never even heard of that. It makes your legs hurt, and that's what keeps you in a wheelchair, though, right?"

"Yeah. I was supposed to be dead when I was forty." She chuckles, pleased by the boundless ignorance of medical science. "Now I'm fifty-three. My brother was real depressed when it got time for him to die, but he didn't neither. I told him, 'Only God knows when you'll die, Chuck, not the doctor.' "

"You mean your brother has this too?"

"Yeah. And two of my sisters. We all in here together."

"You've got a brother and two sisters in this nursing home with you?" My mind just won't quite wrap itself around this information, even as I realize that it's obviously a genetic disease.

"We four got it."

"Do you have other brothers and sisters?"

"There's six more that don't got it."

As Connie and I talk, Hannah is acting agitated and impatient, nosing into the canvas bag of toys, treats, water bowl, and leash I carry around, and dragging out the fleece ball. She tosses it at me, and I reflexively toss it back, wanting to concentrate on Connie's conversation. This is a mistake. Now Hannah won't even think about leaving me alone. I'm struggling with balancing the animal focus and the person focus in this work. Sometimes the residents want to talk and then it seems a shame to refocus them on Hannah. But Hannah needs more training, evidently, so she'll settle down on cue and wait until she's needed again.

"How long have you been here exactly?" I ask Connie, flinging the fleece ball as far as I can, diagonally across the room. It rolls under the other patient's bed and of course I have to retrieve it myself. Hannah barks once, and I bang my head on the bed as I crawl back out in my haste to clamp her mouth closed while I admonish: No barking! Connie's roommate doesn't so much as stir, but Connie's having herself quite a time. "Oh baby, baby, you're so funny," she says and I have a bad feeling she's talking to me rather than Hannah this time.

Trying to recover, I repeat the question. "Uh, you were telling me how long you've been here."

On the tail of a last chuckle she answers, "Umm. I'm fifty-three and . . . ," she says, scrunching her forehead as she calculates, " . . . I think I came in just before I was thirty."

"Was this something you had when you were a child, too? Could you ever walk?" These questions sound too pointed even as I ask them, but Connie seems to be relishing the attention, which is why I persist.

"Used to, only I wobbled. I thought it was the way you're supposed to walk, but then when I went to school, kids said, 'Connie, why you wobble when you walk?' I just didn't pay no attention."

"People, even kids, can be cruel, can't they?"

"Yeah. Sometimes I cried. When I was in my teens, I scooted on the floor. Didn't have no wheelchair, then, but I got around."

"How long did you go to school?"

"Third grade. I wished I could go more." (Evidently, this was well before Public Law 94–142, the Education for Children With Disabilities Act, was passed, though Connie is unfamiliar with this law and can't tell me why she couldn't stay in school.)

"This must have kept you from doing a lot of things you wanted to do."

"I wanted to be married and have me some kids. But life don't always turn out the way you want."

"No, it sure doesn't."

Connie's is one of the larger rooms, mainly because it's intended for three people, but has only two, the now-sleeping roommate in the first bed, and Connie's, in the third, by the window. Where the middle bed would normally be is an empty space. Connie tells me it's because they need extra room for the Hoyer lift, by which the staff get her into and out of bed. There's a television, of course, and some extra touches: a trunk with dogs on it, some plastic flowers, a bulletin board with pictures of Connie and various staff members.

"You must have seen a lot of changes here over the years," I say. "Overall, do you feel this is a good place?"

Connie hesitates. "Pretty good. I was in another place before I came here and this one is better."

"What makes it better?"

"The other place, well, I guess it was worse because they dropped me. Broke my leg."

"They dropped you?" Hannah, who had finally settled down, reacts to the shock in my voice, jumping up and looking around vigilantly for the source of my agitation.

"The girl got mad at me. 'Cause I, well, I messed myself and she had to get me up to change the bed. She dropped me out of the Hoyer lift, moved it too fast because she was mad she had to change the bed. I broke my leg. Ooh, did that hurt. After that I left there, came here. Anyway, this was where my sisters and brother were, and it made it easier for our parents, us bein' in one place."

Sometimes when it's hard to know what to say, Hannah is a big help. How do I word my sadness that such a thing happened to her? Especially when whatever I say will be just a small representation of my real sadness, that the inactivity and changelessness and deprivation of Connie's whole life would feel like a nearly intolerable lull in the progress of my own were I to endure them for a month. I don't have to find words at all, because Hannah noses her way between us and all I have to do is take Connie's hand and help her stroke Hannah's ear.

When we get to Clare's room, she immediately asks me to adjust the air conditioning. I do, of course. Still, although she says, "Thank you, that's fine," her face looks like she's uncomfortable.

"I'm thinking it might be still too hot in here, though. Is it?"

"What's it set on now?"

"The temperature is set on seven and the fan on medium."

"Maybe you could try the fan on high?"

We fiddle back and forth this way until she's more comfortable. "Thank you so much," she says. Her long white braid snakes around the pillow. A tiny blue bow fastens it. "The aide that comes on tonight isn't, uh, very accommodating." She's had to search out an innocuous phrase. As patient and undemanding as Clare is, I glean that this particular aide must ring the bell at the top of the witch meter. "She doesn't like me to ask for things."

"It's no problem at all, Clare. I can do that as many times as you like. We'll leave it this way for now and then, later on when I'm leaving the building, I'll stop back in to see if you want it adjusted again."

I've noticed that Clare has a different roommate, one who's sound asleep at the moment, and I'm wondering where Edwina is. I admit I sometimes ask Edwina about Lucy just so I can hear her get going about how she's going to beat Lucy's goddamn ass. It's a little game we play and it makes me chuckle for days, the image is so magnificently picturesque.

"Where'd Edwina move to?" I ask.

Clare looks flustered. "Oh no, dear, she's dead."

"What? When did she die?" I ask, although it's obvious enough she died while I was gone. Strange how I seek details, as if they somehow give a measure of mastery.

"A couple of weeks ago. A stroke, maybe. They didn't tell me." What must that be like for Clare, I wonder? Bedfast herself, her bed not four feet from Edwina's, privy to each other's most intimate care for years, the only person with whom she talked on a consistent daily basis: Edwina dies and Clare isn't told what happened.

After perhaps twenty minutes with Clare, Hannah and I proceed on to Button's room, giving Big Sam a quick hello on the way. In bed, covered with a black-and-yellow tiger-print spread, Button's face on its matching pillow sham looks diminished, pale. Shelves have been installed on the wall over her small dresser, and more family pictures are displayed, a sure sign that she doesn't expect to leave anytime soon.

"That prick got himself married again," she says as soon as Hannah and I poke our heads in the open door. "Come here, Hannah, come see me. You hungry again?"

I hand Button the bag of food and she starts portioning it out to my chronically ravenous dog.

"Already?" I'm a little stunned because her ex-husband hasn't exactly taken an award for subtlety with this move.

"Couple weeks ago. Asshole. Just didn't want to be married no more, he said. Remember? Wanted to taste the world. Yeah, right." Button's eyes fill but she refuses to break down, distracting herself with Hannah for a couple of minutes. She studies the closest earflap, caresses it over and over, then puts her hand out for Hannah to nuzzle and lick. When she's composed, I hand her the small terrycloth towel I've finally learned to pack rather than have residents wiping their hands on their own clothes after one of my Lab's liberal affection baths.

"Button, I'm so sorry. I know how hurt you must be." And I do; I can read it just by seeing the changes in this woman I've not seen in a month. Her eyes are flatly dark as a night without moon or stars, her skin a yellowish gray, her beautiful nails uneven and unkempt. "Has your daughter brought Precious to see you?"

"No . . . no. I'm not going to see him any more. He's with Rodney and Rodney will take good care of him. I just can't stand it, you know? It's best I let him go. I love him too much. It makes me miss him more than I can bear." Even as she's saying the words, I'm not sure if she's talking about Precious or Rodney, and I cannot bring myself to ask since I suspect the answer is both.

"Well, Hannah will just have to see you more."

Button manages a small smile. "Yes. Bring Hannah more. At least until I move."

"Move?"

"I'm thinking of moving to a nursing home in Tennessee, be near my brothers and sisters. You know, the kids don't have the time to come much, but my brothers and sisters is retired and they'd take me out of a day. Sometimes I go three weeks or a month and never get out of this place at all, and it likes to make me crazy then."

"That's understandable."

"I like to shop, you know, look at things. See the weather."

"Oh Button, I know you'd like to get out more." I hope I sound enthusiastic about the prospect. I wonder if she could go into an Edenizing facility; I wonder if Edenizing facilities take Medicaid. Something for me to look into.

Hannah and I go off looking for Theresa. Instead of strapped into her wheelchair, as usual, she's asleep in bed.

I move on, looking for Liz, but she's in North Carolina visiting her daughter again. A piece of hope that for someone there will be stairs to climb out, that the decline will not be permanent.

On the trails are small signs that indeed, nothing stands still. Whether the change be evolution, devolution, progress or entropy, I realize I need to resist it less, and, rather, to adjust, explore the difference, find what's valuable in it. Already the trails are beginning to heal although there have been two more nights of flooding. Harker's Run has rerouted itself in several places as if it's the receding gumline of the earth itself, trees toppling into the river like loose teeth. Their exposed roots are a strange, bright orange, upended along the bank like a nest of thick-bodied snakes. In several spots, where it once traced the exact edge of the bank, the trail itself is gone, and we are beating a new path six or eight feet back into the woods. I've taken it better this time, as Barb said, bemoaning the losses less and finding what's interesting and intriguing about the river's altered course. The deep pools where the dogs swim are in quite different spots than they were, and we've run into water snakes and a big, black rat snake that coils and draws back to strike.

One day as we hiked the dogs, Barb and I talked about it: the idea of not replaying over and over how it all used to be, but instead keeping an open-enough mind to explore the lessons and beauties of altered terrain. I want to take it as a model for how to approach the life changes, even when they're not chosen changes and seem to have no good in them. Without becoming an insane Pollyanna who trips around in a state of delusional euphoria, it seems as if this mindset is at least a helpful alternative to lapsing into despair and hopelessness.

The very next week, inexplicably, because there's not a great wind or another flood, our beloved grandmother sycamore, its trunk twenty-seven feet in circumference, goes down. Over four hundred years old, in full and undiseased leaf, it just goes down. Broken at about eight feet up from the foot of the tree, we find its bulk crashed to the ground, its true enormity all the more evident as it lies there, dying. I cannot climb onto the fallen trunk, it looms that high and huge in relation to me, at least twice my height as it lies on its side. The trail is way beyond blocked; it has been obliterated. The dogs back up and stare at the aberration. So do I. It is the only time I've seen the forest as a truly dangerous place.

It's Barb who connects the dots. Recent terrorism and war have made it seem as if the world itself might crash and obliterate us all. Most of the Golden View residents take a resigned view. "There's nothing I can do about it," Connie says, shrugging off events I find terrifying. "It's just God's will, I guess."

Her view is shared by more than not. Big Sam watches the news and so does Clare, but Button, like most, is more frustrated than anxious when her soap operas are interrupted by talking heads and hours of "special reports." Those are days they clamor and compete for Hannah, grounded by her simple presence. As am I.

Although the greenery is still full and lush, fall wildflowers are already profuse. A late-blooming phlox, some bright yellow daisy-like blooms called wing stem, and the periwinkle stalk of bells that is giant lobelia edge many of the trails, even some in flooded areas. The meadowy area up near Big Pond is filled with the royal purple of joe-pye weed, black-eyed Susans, and the sharp prickle of lavender thistle. The cattails are deep rich brown over the tall gold of their stems in the shallows there. Up in the pine forest, the center aisle of the cathedral is lined with thick, tall clusters of white snakeroot, their white blooms lacy as Queen Anne's lace and as bridal looking. The air may be dead still, humid, a sticky quilt on our bare arms and legs and faces, and our lungs may rebel at its wet weight, but the earth is not fooled. Cicadas are singing its onward movement. Barb's hip has worsened again, and she has to stop frequently some days, bending at the waist and bracing her hands on her knees. "Though much is taken, much abides; and though we are not now that strength which in old days moved heaven and earth, that which we are, we are. . . ."

Even now.

12. At Their Mercy

Spectacular health is as much a part of my self-image as brown eyes and comparatively short stature, and to my mind just as immutable a fact. I figure I've earned it, too. I exercise over an hour daily, aerobic and/or weight training in addition to my hike with Hannah, and pay attention to nutrition with an emphasis on vegetarian eating. So what if I can't read a telephone book? No sweat. I got myself bifocal contact lenses and I don't even have to acknowledge nearsightedness. When Alan and I went to Nova Scotia, the stiff neck that had been bothering me for a couple of months seemed to get worse with the endlessness of that car ride, so I went to see the doctor when I got home. X-rays showed cervical disk disease. "Could need some traction a couple of times a week," my doctor, also a good personal friend, said casually. "Could keep getting worse, too. Then the only thing to do is surgery."

"Well, *that's* not going to happen, I guaran-damn-tee," I said. "No knives are approaching this neck."

Jim Simcoe is used to my aversion to traditional medicine. "You'll be thrilled to have the surgery if your arm is paralyzed," he said, playing his trump.

Now this was actually something to make me worry a little. My neck was already fairly uncomfortable and some days the discomfort did seem to radiate down my arm. Until I tried one of the new non-steroidal anti-inflammatory drugs. The effect was so dramatic as to nearly convert me to the Church of Medical Science. Unless I forget to take that one little pill daily, and to sleep with three pillows artfully arranged to keep stress off my neck, there's no pain at all. My spectacularly healthy identity continued unchallenged.

Until.

(How many untils will each of us have?)

Until the sultry, stifling evening Alan and I went out to dinner and a summer theater musical with Jim and his wife, Mary, and I had a grand mal seizure just after the overture. And then another seizure.

I woke on the floor of the lobby. Alan and Jim had carried me out, unconscious and seizing, while Mary ran to call for an ambulance. *Yes, I can hear you, yes I know where I am, I'm all right, no lights and sirens, please, please, please. Yes, I feel a little sick, well maybe very sick. Yes, my chest—up toward my shoulder—hurts.* At that, I saw the paramedic signal the driver with a circular hand gesture: lights, siren. So this is what it's like to have a heart attack, I remember thinking. Oh God, I just really don't want this. I have too much to do. Oh—no matter what, do not tell my parents. Do not.

Alan was in the ambulance with me; Jim and Mary followed in their car to the closest hospital, which, unfortunately, isn't one at which Jim is on staff so I had to be under the care of the emergency room physician. I was put on a heart monitor and moved up on the triage list simply because of chest pain. Jim was reassuring as he watched the green lines snake their way up and down hill. He'd taken my pulse and blood pressure as soon as the EMTs arrived, and they'd been fine. Imagine having your own doctor/friend, his RN wife, and your husband with you. Who could have had more caring attention? I obviously wasn't dying, but I was amazed by my own level of fear. I remember my lips and throat desert-dry, croaking out a plea for water. But I couldn't have any water without the ER doctor's permission. I lay on that gurney feeling as if I'd entered a terrible parallel universe in which I was completely at the mercy of someone who hadn't even been in the cubicle to see me yet, and wouldn't for "a while."

Things didn't improve much when he did come in. Chest X-ray. Heart enzymes. CT scan of my head. (Checking for a brain tumor, the nurse kindly explained.) Still no water.

A brain tumor?

"Or an aneurysm," she expanded.

"Anything like this ever happen before?" Jim asked.

No. Well, maybe. Sort of. Yes. Maybe between five and fifteen times. Just never when I was with a doctor. Just when I felt faint and headed for a bathroom where I could faint in privacy. I'd lie down on the floor, hear that roaring in my ears and see the black closing in . . . and a few minutes later I'd just come to.

"The pain?" I asked.

"Probably from the cervical disk disease, but we'll do a stress test next week to be sure," Jim said, after the ER doctor had vanished again. "A heart problem *could* trigger a seizure. We'll just have to see what's up."

The emergency room doctor ordered a "loading dose" of Dilantin, and sent me home. Jim took over, ordering an echocardiogram and stress test, an EEG, and an MRI of my brain (still looking for that lurking brain tumor) and continuing to rule out that the seizure had been triggered by a heart problem. Something that had happened intermittently since childhood (I later listed all the incidents I remembered, a surprising total of seventeen) now loomed with total improbability as a life threatening problem that had been hiding in wait, biding time until it reached out to grab me.

"Don't worry yet," Jim said, again. "Let's just wait and see."

I stink at waiting, it turns out. First there was a maze of appointments, most of which were handled by the head nurse at Jim's office. Another break in my favor, she's a caring and attentive person and also a friend. Even with Sharon managing it, there was confusion. I was scheduled for a closed MRI, something I knew I'd have a lot of trouble with. So we had to call the insurance company, find an approved "open" MRI facility. When Sharon canceled the closed test, the hospital misunderstood and canceled my EEG and stress test, too.

Aside from the inconvenience of all the tests, the disruption of routine, which would have kept me feeling "normal," there was an astonishment of pure fear. It was as though my body had turned into its own terrorist. As I considered a brain tumor versus a heart problem, I started hoping for the heart problem. Not that I want to sound as numbly out-of-control as I felt—or as idiotic—but these episodes that turned out to be seizures had happened occasionally all my life. Logic told me that it was neither of the biggies for which I was being tested.

Logic made no difference. What must it be like for people waiting, waiting, waiting for tests to be scheduled and results to be produced when the likely outcome actually *is* negative? I tried to take hold. "Okay, if this is it, the relative end of spectacular health, then cope." I lectured myself. "Cope, dammit. Who said you should be exempt from what people go through every day?"

Only I couldn't cope. There was that loading dose of Dilantin, followed by daily doses. I was off balance, a little nauseated, light-headed and frequently convinced that another seizure was imminent even though I've previously gone years between them. But I'd never been caught in the churning wheel of American medicine before. I was being "saved" from the remote possibility of another seizure, which would admittedly ruin a day, by Dilantin, which made me feel terrible enough to effectively ruin *every* day.

"This just *has* to be toxic," I insisted. "I can't *walk* straight."

"Don't drive," Jim said and sent me directly to the hospital for yet another blood draw to check my Dilantin level.

"It's high but not toxic," he told me the next day. "Give it time. You'll just have to adjust."

Then the parade of bills began to march to my mailbox. Also the "EOB" (explanation of benefits) statements that look like bills. Most of the bills were wrong. One, for example, said that my insurance company had paid and that I still owed the hospital $1,275, when in fact I owed them my $75 co-payment. Another, for $1,500, was denied on the grounds that I'd not had the MRI at an approved facility, although even the insurance company had it in their computer that I'd called to find out where to go and had, indeed, used the facility to which they'd sent me. In all, I made five calls to two hospitals and a total of six calls to my insurance company. Each call involved navigating a telephone menu of multiple steps before I could speak with a person. I have no question that my aged and ailing mother who goes limp in response to technology would have despaired and written out checks, convinced that "All that's on their computers, they know what we owe; we'll get bad credit if we don't pay; my, wasn't *that* expensive."

Here's the point: I'm young, compared to my parents and to most of Hannah's and my patients at Golden View. I'm probably unusually fit, unusually healthy. I have a graduate degree. Simply put, I have power I was able to use. I researched seizures, seizure medications, seizure triggers. Ultimately I told my doctor what (lower) dose of Dilantin I could handle, settling for less than optimal protection in order to be able to function. We talked for forty minutes about seizure prevention and he respected my autonomy. What had actually happened to me were grand mal seizures that didn't indicate a thing beyond a seizure disorder that just hadn't been diagnosed before. It was in fact, no big deal.

But it surely did give me a taste of what Theresa, for example, experiences as she has test after test. It helped me understand what Big Sam's waiting feels like. It surely put me in touch with the unbelievable hoops and worries of all the forms, all the computer-generated bills, and with how difficult it is to find a person to talk at the end of a chain of telephone "menus." I came to realize how heavily I depended on Alan, his help, his support, which made me feel infinitely tender toward Mary's length of loneliness. I thought of Button's longing for the comfort of her Precious as Hannah stretched herself alongside me when I felt badly enough that I laid down. How will I be able to give my parents enough help, when as small an incident as this was in the grand scheme caused so much turmoil and difficulty?

As I've said, this wasn't the first time I've experienced my body's betrayal, only the most dramatic and undeniable. After that last seizure, I took stock of the little facts I've stuck like dusty knick-knacks up in my mental attic. There's that cervical disk disease. The antacids I pop after certain meals that never, ever bothered me a decade ago. The bags under my eyes, the same eyes that can't read a phone book. The wrinkles on my neck, the parentheses that frame my mouth. I have trouble deciding which of my chins is my least favorite. Many days I have no idea whatsoever where my car keys are or why I wanted them in the first place. Every now and then I remember how I viewed my parents when they are the exact age I am now. *Old.*

As I struggled with the aftermath, I was startled to realize that my children see me that way: already *old.* Of course, Hannah doesn't see any of that. All she reacts to is what counts, the kindness on my face, for example, rather than the spreading wrinkles. In fact, the single best memory I have from the tangle of unpleasant experiences connected with that last seizure comes from Hannah.

Our daughter had left her little beagle with us for a couple of weeks while she traveled, and it was during the time she was gone that I took my joy ride in the ambulance. A few days later, home and reeling from too much Dilantin one morning, I suddenly felt the aura that precedes a seizure and laid down flat as Jim had told me to. Copper, Brooke's beagle, immediately trotted over and jumped on my stomach. My sister Jan was visiting then. Seeing me try to move Copper aside, she shouted at Copper to get off me. Hurrying into the room, Alan saw both problems, and also started yelling at Copper to get off. Copper wasn't having any of it. A classic lap-lover, he thought he'd just settle on my abdomen and have himself a nice nap.

Almost simultaneously with the barrage of ineffective shouting, Hannah appeared and sprang into action. She barked at Copper once and then literally nosed him off me. There was one more bark as she moved in behind and drove him, efficient as a horse driving cattle, onto an adjacent couch. She then stationed herself between Copper and me while Copper huddled, utterly obedient to her after ignoring three adult humans. Hannah stayed unmoving, guarding me, until I was able to stand up and release her. Only then did she in turn release Copper.

I would not have predicted that she would so completely assess a new situation, grasp what was needed, and come to my assistance, nor could I have foreseen how it would touch me, the gratitude I would feel. Once again, the therapy dog does her best work with her own person. I would not have guessed the comfort of her, how her presence obviates the need for explanations or pleas. When fear crowds my mind as it does so much now—this new sense of my own vulnerability, my parents far away and in need, the world swaying drunkenly as it walks the line between all-out war and its lesser versions—she is here, she is with me.

13. Life Goes On

Leaves thin, light enters the forest. Day by day, more light, clear, gilt, filtered by the thinning, gilding leaves. Late September. The earth's spin guns its motor toward winter after August's long stifled sigh.

By month's end, in some lights and where maples tower over small, tucked-in houses, my town looks as if scarlet flames will shortly consume it. But in the woods, the canopy is mostly yellow even if the poison ivy is deep red as it vines up tree trunks. When the autumn breeze rouses, big green walnuts and Osage oranges thud on the ground; sometimes they scarcely miss our heads. When Hannah hears one fall, she charges forward to investigate. Barb and I madly try to catch a falling leaf as it whirligigs its way down. She claims it's absolutely proven to produce good luck and I could use some. All we succeed in doing is making ourselves dizzy while the dogs abandon squirrel-chasing in favor of staring at this new madness of ours.

In Harker's Run, the water is as crystalline as I've ever seen it. Where it pools into the dogs' deep swimming holes, fat, flat leaves float on the surface and in the slant light of four o'clock, their perfect shadows lie on the sandy riverbed beneath. Then the water hurries on, turning white over the rocky little falls, singing its way on and on, stream to river, river to sea, the poignant vibrato of leaving.

An ache of blue sky over yellow woods. The nose and throat tang of leaf-fall. My Hannah, leaping like a stag, bounding her zigzag trail revisions, exuberant, running as high and fast as her blood, chasing anything, harming nothing. October. The honeysuckle underbrush is thinner now, but still wholly green. First to leaf in the spring, last to brown in the fall. It's as if spring rises skyward off the earth and summer is a long breath before the reverse of autumn. Hannah has progressed from breaking up softball games, chasing fly balls with greater speed and efficiency than any left fielder, to, most recently, decimating a soccer game by charging into the fray, stealing the ball and nosing it down the field exactly as a player, only substituting the two sides of her nose for two insteps, and streaking toward the goal to the hysterical laughter of the two college teams. Sometimes her obedience isn't exactly what it might be. I apologized, but both teams brushed it off in their haste to make competitive recruitment offers.

At Golden View, as the United States inflicts more damage, more of the residents mention the world situation. The men shape weak fists and pump them remembering the big war and how they won it. Instead of having their helplessness mirrored in the television, there are images of power, and those postwar memories are good. Some have relatives being called to active duty, grandsons for the most part, and one granddaughter. Pride and defiance illuminates most of those faces, fret and worry on a few others. Still, in this world set aside from the world, there is little talk of war. Bingo numbers are being called as the Fire Engine Lady chants on.

The scuttlebutt here is that Carla has been promoted to activity director. It's Megan who hastens to tell me this, doubtless because of our previous conversation about the murky nature of Judy's doings. Megan and I smile, conspirators in our assessment that this is, indeed, excellent news. Judy, who's an RN, has gone back to the day shift on C wing. I pass her on my way to Liz's room; she's wearing an old-fashioned white nurse's uniform complete with bobby-pinned-on cap with spit curls down the sides of her face. I turn my disbelieving doubletake and involuntary grin into a cheery greeting and keep moving. Judy's outfit will make Mary, for one, very happy.

"I've just been stewing in my own juices too long," Liz says. "I'm getting into petty stuff, you know? I'm down to one nerve and the people who sit at my table at dinner—the seats are assigned, you know—are stepping on it. So much stupid gossip. Sally, she just drives me up the wall, she goes on and on about her every little complaint. Of course, here I am doing the same thing."

"What's happening with your discharge planning? I mean, have you talked to the social worker?" Hannah sighs and plops on the floor without being told to. She must be able to sense when I'm in a talking mode here, a big disappointment to her since when I'm talking she's not garnering treats from anyone.

Liz looks down shamefacedly. "Uh, no. I haven't. I mean, I've seen him, but I haven't had the nerve to ask. What's that meeting called?"

"The case conference?"

"Yeah. It does sort of make me mad that I'm supposed to be notified and get to be there."

"It's your right, Liz. I'll come and support you and help you ask questions if you like. But you need to find out about it. They won't tell me. They *shouldn't* tell me, you know? Because of confidentiality."

She nods. Her dark hair has been bobbed since I last saw her. Now it's a little below ear-length, unruly curls tamed with a headband. She's wearing a gray T-shirt and sweatpants. I found her in the "smoking lounge," a tiny, ill-ventilated room with two chairs, a lamp, some piled-up boxes and jumbled junk, and a coke machine. Every now and then a staff member comes in and feeds the machine, which coughs and hawks out a soda. Liz speaks to each by name and they are pleasant in return, most bending to play a bit with Hannah who scarcely rouses herself, sensing, I'm sure, that food won't be involved.

"How did it go at your daughter's?" This is the first time I've seen her since she returned from another trial visit to her married daughter's home, which happens to be in North Carolina. I haven't told her that's where my parents live, but I've certainly thought about the coincidence: we two women, the same age, engaging in passionate discussions about dogs, hair coloring and the like, meeting at Golden View in such disparate circumstances. We travel to the same distant state, she hoping to be cared for by her child, and I hoping to give care to my mother. Sometimes I see my life as a coin, long ago balanced on edge, which could have fallen with either side up. When I'm around Liz, though, another image haunts me. I think perhaps all our lives are connected in mysterious ways, and she and I are two sides of that coin still balanced on edge and rolling to North Carolina.

"Oh it was okay," she says, answering my question about the trip.

"Just okay?"

"I kept waiting for the shoe to drop."

I have no idea what she means, and say so.

"Oh, you know, the 'see what you did to yourself? We tried to tell you, but you're too dumb to listen and look where you've ended up and it's all your own fault' stuff. It's all true, so it's not like I can argue the point."

"So did she say it?" I'm hoping the answer is no.

"Oh not really. But I knew. They'd talk about things that are going to happen in the future and make it clear that I'm not going to be there. It was like, well, *you're not going to be available*. I have no idea why I'm not going to be available. They must be sending me someplace."

"Liz, you have a right to know these things," I say softly, rabble-rousing but trying not to sound like it. I grin at her and start playing tug-of-war with Hannah to soften just how serious I am. "Get a backbone and stir up some trouble!" What I'm thinking is that something or someone has to challenge her to take hold.

"I know I need to," she says ruefully, burying her face in Hannah's neck. "I could do it for someone else. I just can't do it for myself."

"This could be when that split personality gets handy, then."

Liz snorts a laugh. "It's about time there was a use for my evil twin."

This is when I am most tempted to get on my high horse and engage in passionate preaching about the need for a Patient Advocate, and my motive is again, simple. Mom. Dad. Peter. Any and all of the people I love. It frightens me to think of any of us absorbed into the great baffle of this system, and I mean baffle in the sense of confusion as well as something that silences.

That baffle has already started to engulf us, though: Mom's doctor left a message on my answering machine late yesterday afternoon. "Lynne, your mother fell again this morning and your Dad couldn't lift her. She's been taken to the hospital by ambulance. I think it's time for a face-to-face meeting. You, your sister, your parents, and I all need to meet and make some decisions about long term care. Or getting a lot more help in the home. Your Dad can't cope with this."

By the time I'd returned Dr. Fretwell's call, reached Jan, and we'd tracked down which hospital Mom had been taken to, she was just out of X-ray. The next piece of news really threw me: she'd been admitted to the hospital but refused to stay. Adamantly.

"Can you handle this?" the doctor later reported asking Dad dubiously. The X-rays showed two broken ribs, and a broken clavicle.

"I'll sure do my best," he'd answered. "I think so." And so they left, Mom in a sling, black and blue, bandaged. In the middle of the night, I was sleepless, suddenly·remembering the intensity of the pain of broken ribs if you cough. My mother has a chronic cough that occasionally stretches into an interminable half-hour and leaves her exhausted. First thing this morning, I called the airline to trade in some of the frequent flyer miles I've been hoarding for emergencies, only to discover that I can't use them until next week; the limit of "award" seats have been already booked. (Since Mom is neither in the hospital nor dead, the airline won't allow the use of discount seats without booking and paying fourteen days in advance. It is over $900 if I don't use the frequent flyer miles; I surely won't be able to do *that* too often. I'm never sure when it just can't wait. This time, Dr. Fretwell says to come next week. How *can* that be all right, though?)

Splats of cold stuttering rain took down more of the leaves in the past couple of days. On the trails, they lie in bright splotches of yellow accented here and there by scarlet, a patchwork quilt on top of the longer-down ones that have been walked flat as dun sheets. Now, it's almost as if the ground is competing with the canopy for which has the most color. The underbrush, though, is still purely green.

Outside Mary's window, the one she faces from both bed and the blue easy chair that squats beside the pillow, is a crab tree. It's not very healthy, she tells me. "Look, not a leaf on it. It's too soon for them all to be down. And the birds won't touch those crabapples. They come and peck once and then they take off."

As she talks Mary is playing with Hannah and her miserable fleece ball. I say miserable because as she scrambles on the shiny tiles to fetch it, the ball has several times ended up deep beneath Mary's bed and Hannah can't squeeze herself under to retrieve it. Unfortunately, I can.

"Well, it's pretty clean under here anyway," I say as I lie on my belly, head turned sideways to fit, and wriggle myself backward with the ball. Hannah snatches the ball from my hand and drops it in Mary's lap. The room is so crammed that I bump the TV table, the bed and Mary's knees as I get back to my feet.

"You don't say," she says. "Call Peter Jennings. That belongs on the *World News Tonight.*"

Someone from the local Catholic church has brought her a bird feeder. A suet cake of seeds is suspended from it. Mary is very pleased. "The birds don't like that crab tree," she says again. "It's not healthy. But then not much here is. I didn't think they'd let her put up a bird feeder outside my window. They let me have it, though. They're awfully nice to me sometimes. I don't know why, because I have a lot of complaints."

And within a minute, she's launching into one. "The administrator we have now is just awful," she says with heavy emphasis on the *aw*. She touches her short, straight white hair, which is, as always, neatly brushed, back from her face. Then she fingers one hearing aid, adjusting the volume deftly. "I've been here almost ten years now, and he's the worst one yet. If I could, I'd kick his ass right out of here."

"Sounds like you don't like him much," I say inanely. I'm trying to be careful about saying anything negative about the staff so it never gets back to them that I did. The deeper I get into this, the more I hear and I'm making an effort to limit my rabble-rousing to Liz, since she seems the best candidate to make it out.

On the subject of the administrator, Mary rolls her eyes at the obviousness of my brilliant conclusion that she doesn't like him much. "He doesn't talk to us. He doesn't even look at us. He stands in the entrance to the dining room and watches us, but he doesn't say a word and he looks over our heads, not *at* us. Never a single smile. What's the matter with him?"

I treat the question as rhetorical. Meanwhile, Mary is feeding Hannah kibble, a piece at a time to make it last. "You're not even chewing that," she scolds Hannah. "Don't rush through it. You'll be old soon enough." She looks at me, then, as she considers what she's said. "I surely never thought I'd be here ten years," she says softly. "I'm grateful my husband died when he did. He hated it here and he was only here a matter of weeks. I'll never forget how he looked at me and said 'look what you've gotten us into now,' but you know, he was the reason we were in here to begin with. He was too sick for me to take care of alone. So then he dies, wouldn't you just know it, and *I'm* the one who is stuck here forever then. I thought I'd go to my son's, but that didn't work out. Oh, I don't mean to speak bad of my husband. He was a good man. Selfish, but good . . . just *selfish*."

I am, of course, thinking of Mom and Dad as Mary tells this story. Still waiting to get to them with my frequent flyer miles, I'm thinking of my frustration, to be honest. This morning, I got another call from Mom's doctor, who has arranged a home health care aide and the delivery of a nebulizer because she's concerned about pneumonia setting in. When I talk to him, Dad sounds as wrung out as a used-up sponge yet keeps insisting, "I can take care of her." I realize uneasily why this sounds so familiar: Helen took care of Peter at home until she was on the verge of collapse and her son showed up to intervene and get Peter into Golden View. *Why* wouldn't Mom stay in the hospital? What could she have been thinking? Am I angry on Dad's behalf or my own?

As she talks, Mary keeps caressing Hannah's head, which Hannah has plunked in her lap. Right after she pronounces her late husband *selfish* for the last time, she grabs Hannah's whole head and neck in what the Delta Society and Therapy Dogs International refer to as a "restraining hug." "Oh I love you, girl, I love you, I love you," she repeats, her Hannah mantra, while my dog stands quietly to give her time.

Hannah and I haven't seen Big Sam in a while, so we leave Mary and head to the common area where he usually parks. Today the space is literally crowded with residents. I'm struck again by the torpor that seems to have replaced air. The October afternoon is pure Indian summer, and yellow and rust chrysanthemums, donated by a church in town, have livened the courtyard. Some pumpkins have been set out, part of a decorative yard arrangement of corn stalks and Indian corn. No one is outside, no one is talking to anyone else, not even residents like Big Sam who will carry on an animated conversation with me. I notice that everyone's face lights with interest as Hannah precedes me into the area and begins sniffing the carpet, ever hopeful that people were messy at lunch.

"So what's been going on?" I ask as I dig the damn fleece ball back out of the canvas bag. At least out here, there's no bed for it to get stuck under. Medicine carts, walkers, wheelchairs, sure, but at least no bed.

"Not a damn thing," he says with a shrug. Then, slyly, he adds: "I might be gettin' outta here is all."

"And you call *that* 'not a damn thing'?" I say in mock exasperation. Sam gets distracted by a tug-of-war with Hannah over the damn fleece ball, ducking his head to hide that he's chuckling. "So how is this coming about, and if you don't tell me now I'm taking that ball away from both of you!"

Hannah backs up two steps, reacting to my threat to take the ball away, which amuses Sam. "Okay, okay," he says. "My sister-in-law is looking into getting meals on wheels for me, so I can go home. I'm getting a cordless phone so I can always keep it with me, and, you know, if I get into trouble, I can call for help."

"Hey, Big Sam, that's just great news. Is, um, this the doctor's idea or . . ."

"He just keeps sayin', 'you live alone.' Like I don't know that!" Sam chuckles. "Duh! So I live alone. I'll have food and I'll have a phone and my sister-in-law is gonna check on me every day. I can't wait to get out of here."

So, with not one thing changing in Sam's physical capacity, after almost two years here, Big Sam is looking forward to going home. What it took, apparently, was a relative finally willing to make some calls, come up with a half-way reasonable plan, *appear* to be taking responsibility, *et voilà*. Sam is sprung. Initiative plus pushing equals home. There is a help van with a wheelchair lift operated by the senior citizens center in town if he needs a ride, and there are social activities and excursions planned and operated by the same center. I'll bring in all that information to Sam, in case no one else does.

We're trying to head toward the desk where I sign out, but we run into Carla and a resident I've not seen before. A black man who looks to be in his mid-forties, stick-thin, in a half-reclining position in a motorized wheelchair because the legs are raised, cushioned on a bed pillow, in fact. One foot is slightly drawn up and the toes pointed in; the arm on the same side of his body is likewise disabled, the wrist bent on itself as if broken. A white hand towel hangs from the man's mouth. I guess that he's unable to speak, both because of the towel and because when Carla talks to him the questions and comments are rhetorical. At one point he lets the towel drop but still doesn't speak. Then, with his good hand, he picks the towel up and replaces it. Is it there so he won't drool? There's no one I can ask at the moment, though Carla clearly is accustomed to seeing it.

I regret that I'm still awkward in these situations, not more or less so than others, but that's the point and the reason I push myself to enter them. How often do we avoid talking to people with disabilities, dreading that we'll be unable to understand their response and not know what to say next? That must contribute to their isolation. I'm learning to be patient and light in my approach, but nonetheless, to be sure I *do* approach.

At any rate, I learn by listening to Carla that the man's name is Dan. He watches Hannah intently and uses his good hand to motor closer to her. Trooper that she is, she neither barks nor backs up though this is her first experience with a motorized wheelchair on the move toward her. If I'd had to judge by her reaction to a vacuum cleaner at home, I'd have expected her to treat it like an invading creature from outer space and yelp a red alert to the greater tri-state area. Instead, she stands still, tail swinging.

"Dan, would you like to play with Hannah?" Carla asks.

Dan just looks at her, but Carla knows how to read his face. She gets Hannah's fleece ball and puts it in Dan's good hand. Dan tosses it diffidently and Hannah, of course, retrieves it. She tries to put it on his feet, which are, to her mind I imagine, stuck out in front of him like hands. Carla gets the ball off Dan's feet and hands it to him. The whole process is repeated two more times, each of Dan's pitches a little stronger, a little farther. Carla's long curls swing out in front of her face each time she bends to pick up the ball. We're in the hallway adjacent to the nursing station on L wing, where Liz's room is, and a small crowd of staff and residents is collecting to watch. I see that Dan notices them. His eyes, black in this dim hallway light, dart up to take them in and then go back to Hannah several times.

"Carla, try angling the chair so that Hannah can put it in his lap," I suggest. "She'll drop it there if she can get to it." I know this from watching Hannah play with Big Sam.

Carla moves Dan's chair and Hannah begins dropping the fleece ball directly into Dan's lap so that no one else need be involved; he can play with Hannah on his own.

Everything changes then. Dan begins lifting the ball over his head and waving it back and forth before he throws it, which makes Hannah do a little eagerness dance, her eyes laser-fixed on her beloved, miserable damn ball.

"Don't tease her, Dan," Carla cautions.

The light in the hallway is late afternoon, further muted by having gone through windows, around partitions. Dan's face and hands are the shade of coffee, white pillows behind his head as well as beneath his legs and feet, white towel hanging from his mouth and swinging with the motion of his brown hand as it holds the white fleece ball. The chocolate Lab is in front of him, feet planted wide as she anticipates the toss, head up, ears forward, tail swinging in great wide wags. It is a portrait in tones of brown, amber and white. As I take it in, Hannah begins to match the swing of her tail to the motion of Dan's hand.

Finally, Dan pitches the ball the farthest yet. Hannah tears off to retrieve it. Wary staff are starting to move idle medical paraphernalia littering the hall out of the way. Dan watches from behind those silent eyes, slightly narrowed now with some inscrutable anger. He picks up the ball Hannah deposits in his lap and waves it above his head again. Then he pretends to throw it. Hannah tears off, quickly realizes he's not released the ball, and spins to face him, waiting for it.

Dan pretends again. Hannah begins prancing up and down, little jumps of excitement. Dan pretends again and Hannah barks, once.

"Dan, don't tease her," Carla says.

Dan continues, upping the ante by pretending to throw the ball behind him.

"Dan . . ."

It seems for all the world as if he's just being cruel. Carla is getting peeved and I'm concerned about his frustrating Hannah deliberately. Hannah, though, seems unperturbed. After the single bark, she continues to wait for Dan's throw while he teases, pretends and fakes over and over. Finally, I get it. How could I have forgotten that first nursing home lesson? *Power.* What has Dan had power over lately? Only this one big-hearted dog who drops the ball in his lap, on the side of his good arm, so no one has to help him. Dan is running this show.

"Hannah has kind eyes, doesn't she?" Liz said before Hannah and I left her in the smoking lounge today. Then she put her arms around me. Indeed, Hannah has kind eyes, but one of the amazing gifts of animal-assisted therapy is the way the residents confuse me with my Hannah, the affection and appreciation and trust that spills over onto the human who brings them this good, good dog.

14. The Root of Evil

October now: sunny-cool days, shorter and shorter as they gather momentum, tumbling toward winter. Hannah and Betty prance, chasing balls and each other, relishing the serrated edge on the air, the chilly water. Hannah seeks out spots where the bank is elevated to do her splay-legged exuberant belly flop, while Betty takes the sane route into the river or Big Pond, where the water is framed with golding cattails and every shade of autumn is mirrored on its glassy surface. The beavers never did fell the big tree they were working on; there's a wedge out of it more than halfway through.

The canopy is entirely down except for a few amber-gold oak trees that guard the far side of Harker's Run at the top of the ravine. Yesterday, in the sand edging one of the dogs' swimming holes, those oaks so far above it they seemed to pierce the sky, Barb and I found fresh, clear deer tracks right at the spot where, last week, we'd come upon a dead buck, his beautiful body apparently unmarked. We'd guessed a bullet hole was hidden beneath him. He was just feet from the easy slope into clean water, where the little river pools just so for drinking and swimming below the song of rapids and the sigh of sheltering trees. Since then, Hannah and Betty have intently nosed the spot where he'd been; we don't know if a hunter returned for the body or if, during the night of heavy rain that followed the discovery, the river carried it away. I've also found a plastic bag of ammunition on the trail, not a big enough gauge to take a deer's life, but enough to kill a bird or squirrel. No hunting signs are at every entry to the forest, but when people want something badly enough, no signs, no warnings, no legal or moral laws seem to make much difference. The deer haven't been as evident this fall, overall; Hannah has given her glorious yipping chase to far fewer than she flushed from their daytime nests last fall. "It was a harsh winter last year," Hardy reminded me. "The deer population took a hit from starvation, too."

The headlong tumble toward winter is being repeated in several realms. Peter has been moved from Golden View to the hospital and, finally, into hospice care where now multiple neighbors and friends are helping Helen keep a vigil. And I feel it too as I head to North Carolina, to the meeting Mom's doctor has requested to discuss "the situation." In the days that have elapsed since Dr. Fretwell's call, I've overheated phone wires trying to lend support and perform long-distance micromanagement. My success rate has been thoroughly humiliating, and I'm convinced again that being on the scene is crucial. I've cleared my calendar though; this time I'm prepared to stay at least a week.

When I arrive from the airport, a little early, both my parents begin to cry. Dad has Mom propped up against their bathroom counter, and he's dressing her in a bright aqua pants and top outfit. I'm afraid to hug her close and fully, the way I want to, that's how frail, how breakable she looks. I put my arms around the two of them, the three of us supported by the corner between wall and counter. I don't want them to see that I'm crying. Mom's white hair hasn't been done since before the accident, and she's upset about it, poking at errant ends that refuse to hold their curl. She didn't want me to see her like this, she says. I couldn't care less what her hair looks like; what I care about are the broken bones and dark bruises, the new hollows dark as knotholes in her cheeks and under her eyes, although she sleeps hours of each day and all night, too. My mother has sky-blue eyes, her trademark, and almost always dresses in blue to highlight them. Today her eyes look grayish, as does her skin.

The next five days are a blur of arguing with Dad about whether we need a ramp for Mom's wheelchair (he says no, I insist yes and one is built in the garage, too steep because they won't agree to putting one at the front door). I'd not even known she was back in a wheelchair; nobody had mentioned that on the phone. I get a bedside commode, a gait belt to ease the transfer from chair to toilet to bed, a toilet seat riser, a shower chair. Medicare pays only for the commode. "I don't care," I say. "We need these and I'm getting them."

A physical therapist comes to the house, as does an Occupational

Therapist Mom's doctor wants to conduct an assessment of what modifications may be needed for the house. Dad stalks out of the peach and beige living room, where I've tried to make nice and serve iced tea while we have a good productive discussion, as best as one can stalk with a heavy limp. He thinks the OT is "a phony."

Throwing up his hands, he has a minor explosion after she leaves. "We were just fine. We had a nice life until Mom fell, and now she's recovering. We'll be just fine again. We don't need all this." The blatant implication is that everything was just ducky until I blew into town. He leaves again when the person from HealthMates comes to install the call button necklace for Mom to wear around her neck, and he's almost rude to the Senior Care Services representative as she explains the support system of companion and respite care, laundry, housekeeping, and nursing available from her private agency. I'd called them at the doctor's suggestion. "Mom's recovering," Dad reiterates. "I can take care of her. I don't need help." Right now, he's doing everything himself: house, cooking, laundry, yard. A cleaning lady comes in twice a month.

That evening, I dash to pick up the phone in the kitchen. Mom is watching a movie in the bedroom as Dad dozes in front of TV sports in the living room. Helen is calling on the TDD phone she's gotten for the hearing impaired. I can hear her voice, but my answers get transcribed and appear in writing on a screen for her, and I keep forgetting to say "go ahead," to let the transcriptionist know I'm finished speaking.

Peter has just died. He was peaceful, she was with him, and several friends were at the hospital with her. I feel badly that I wasn't. The memorial service will be after I get home. I hang up, wipe some tears. Godspeed, Peter. Bless you, Helen. I didn't manage to say any of the right things to her, whatever they might have been. I wonder what it's like at home tonight. On the coast of North Carolina, it's warm, clear, richly moonlit. I go out on the porch for a moment and watch the running lights of a small boat as it passes the house. Its wake laps against our dock. A good night for travel.

Everything Helen did, for so long and so alone, my father is doing now. She always believed Peter might come home. Just the way Dad says Mom will recover and their lives will be as they were. But whose is it to take away hope? Mine? And whose is it to say what can happen and what may?

We meet with Mom's doctor in her office one unseasonably hot afternoon. How can Dad expect to get Mom around by himself in a wheelchair? It's been exhausting for the two of us to get her from house to car, car to waiting room, waiting room to doctor's conference room, where a big white marker board still has notes from a staff meeting posted. Dad's face is grim and frustrated; I know he thinks this meeting is a crock. He thinks it was all my idea, too.

Dr. Fretwell is about my age, fair and freckled, with short reddish-brown hair and a thick wave of bangs across her forehead. She'll brush them aside as she pushes her glasses into place when she looks up from consulting Mom's chart.

She hugs Mom who's bandaged, in her wheelchair, and pale as her pastel blue top, though she's put on lipstick again for the first time today, and asks how she's doing before we start business. It's clear Dr. Fretwell has Dad's number. "I'm not automatically opposed to denial. It can strengthen our spirits and will and backbone, keep us actively in there fighting. I'm not opposed to it until it starts doing some harm. You're crossing that line, now," she says, aiming her words clearly. Then she reads Mom's chart to him. Each fall is documented, as are multiple calls from Dad about which Jan and I didn't even know.

"Your daughters are right. You've got to get more help. When a caregiver can't get a night's sleep or respite, the patient ends up in a nursing home." She leans across the conference table and says it directly to Dad, who's opposite her.

"I'll take it under advisement," responds the Colonel, arms crossed over his chest, never breaking eye contact.

"That's code for no," I insert. Jan's voice chimes in to back me up, otherworldly but strong, on the speakerphone from her office hundreds of miles distant. "That's definitely code for no." Even Mom nods affirmatively.

Dad doesn't bother to deny it.

Mom's largely quiet through the whole meeting. She hasn't fought getting the call button necklace, most likely because after the fall that broke her clavicle and ribs, she fell again before I got here, while

Dad was out getting groceries and doing errands he'd put off. He'd left her with the wireless phone in her lap, but she tried to get from her wheelchair into the bathroom by herself instead of calling the neighbor as he'd told her to. Unable to reach the phone, she lay on the floor over three hours. I remember how Herman cried for help for fifteen minutes after the fall that put him in the hospital. "Three hours is a long, long time. I just prayed," Mom told me of the incident. That's my mother speaking, who's never mentioned any religious beliefs of her own. And she loves the chamberpot, the toilet riser seat, the gait belt that allows her to be assisted from the waist rather than being pulled up by her good arm. She won't say how she feels about more help coming in. I'm terribly concerned that the issue is money: neither one of them want to spend it on help although they have the resources. But, too, there's pride, determination to remain independent, and an element of Depression-era self-reliance and military duty in Dad. He'd scoff at both words, but Jan and I see how stubbornness and heroism blur each other.

The meeting ends with no decisions. I realize I have pushed as hard as I can before it all starts to boomerang. It probably already has, if truth be told. Perhaps Dad will consider what he's heard and make a different decision about our bringing in more help in a week or two, when he has time to feel like it's his idea. Or he won't.

I leave feeling heartbroken and guilty. I know Dad's angry at me for what I've done, even as I realize I'm simply the bull's-eye on the reality target right now. How can I blame him for being angry at the physical diminishments, the fragility, the pain, the fear they both feel? And in spite of all that was accomplished while I was with Mom and Dad, I travel home with a sense of failure in my suitcase, and it's heavy. Maybe I've alienated Dad; maybe he thinks it's I who have diminished him.

From the airport, I drive to Barb's where Hannah has been spending the daytimes of my absence. In my mind, I foresee her wild happiness at my return, feel her licking my face at the top of each of the joy leaps.

But no. It turns out she's mad at me, too. She barely glances in my direction then turns, deliberately, it seems, to give Barb an affectionate nuzzle. When I try to hug her, she slips her head out of my arms. My absence has wounded her, even as my presence, or more truly, what my presence stood for, has wounded my father. This is going to take some time to heal all around.

"Don't worry about it," Barb said with reference to Hannah's attitude. "She's probably still a bit drunk, anyway."

"Drunk?"

"I left a big bowl of red grapes on the kitchen counter when I went to aerobics yesterday. When I came home, Hannah slunk to me with her ears folded back and a very guilty look on her face. Then I found the kitchen floor covered with grape stems, but not one grape anywhere. Apparently, she prefers a young red vintage. Probably if you put a nice merlot in her water bowl tonight, she'll forgive you for leaving her."

"How are your plans to move to Tennessee coming?" I ask Button, hoping to surprise her with the information I have stuffed in my back pocket about Edenizing facilities that take Medicaid. Outside, the sky is pure periwinkle and the last leaves are sun-gilt, luminous. A great V of migrating sand cranes passed overhead earlier. Northern birds that stand waist-high to a human, the pipers flew so high they looked like swallows from where we stood.

When I'd entered her room, Button was asleep, but I spoke anyway because I truly thought she was about to fall out of bed. Her head was hanging over the side almost exactly as Hannah lays, her head always off her bed, inches lower than her body when she's stretched out in her deepest sleep. And, I rationalized, Button hates to miss a chance to fondle Hannah's ears and let Miss Ever-Ravenous coax kibble from her hand a piece at a time.

Button just shakes her head no. "I don't think I'll be doing that."

"Oh Button, what's happened?"

She's evasive at first, caressing Hannah who nuzzles her hand and arm, but she keeps starting sentences of explanation, and I sense she wants to talk about it.

"I can't ex . . . there's a lot to the story. I mean, nobody knows. . . . Oh no, I don't mean to cry," she adds fumbling around her night table for a tissue.

"You can cry, Button, it won't bother me at all. And if you want to talk about something, I won't tell anyone." I pull three or four tissues from the box and tuck them in her hand. Hannah sits with her chest against the mattress and lays her head on Button's thigh. Button's sheets are that striped tiger print again, olive and brown, and Hannah's head looks like part of the pattern.

"I haven't got a cent to my name, not a cent, not a cent. See, when you come in here, you can't have any money to your name." She's referring, of course, to Medicaid, and I do know that many people desperately try to "spend down" their money in order to qualify for Medicaid and not to have to pay for nursing home care themselves.

I nod that I understand this dilemma.

"I don't know how someone's supposed to go the rest of her life on nothing, but I kept some, you know, after Rodney did what he did, that prick." Anger perks her up for a moment and there's life in her eyes, but it doesn't last. "I had seven thousand five hundred dollars cash that I'd kept out, and I gave it to my daughter Leann to keep for me, so I wouldn't be helpless, you know? I gave her my car and she was supposed to just put the money in her name but keep it for me for when I could get out of here. Now she won't give me any of it. She's got a block on her phone so I can't call her, and she won't give me any money at all. Not a cent. I haven't got a single penny." Tears are coursing down Button's cheeks now. When I look closely, I see how gray-yellow her skin is and how sunken her eyes, dull, and seeming as if a thumb has smudged charcoal above and below them.

"Oh Button, isn't this the daughter who's really close to you? She's the one who brought Precious to see you when you were first here, right? Your own daughter, not one of the stepdaughters?"

"Yeah, she used to come, but I haven't seen her for five weeks now. And I haven't a cent to my name." Button repeats it over and over, as if she's trying to make it compute, which it never does.

"What do you think has happened?"

"I think she spent it."

"Might some of your other children step in and try to help you?" I'm grasping at straws, I realize, even as I speak. If this daughter of Button's has spent or taken off with her money, it's obvious enough that Button is stuck. She's had to declare herself essentially penniless—and powerless—to get Medicaid. She'd be calling herself a liar.

"The other ones are far away. Texas and California and Michigan. They don't really know what's going on." It's distance adding another dimension to the problem, the same issue I bump into over and over with my own parents. And it's the one I fear as my adult children stretch into their freedom to "settle anywhere," as college and graduate school graduation dates pop out on the calendar like wildflowers in April.

"Button, I'm so sorry." It's utterly completely inadequate and yet I can't think of another thing to say. "You must be terribly hurt and discouraged."

"I just feel like this is my last road. My last road."

"Things may still change. Try not to give up hope."

Button shakes her head. "I just think this is my last road."

Hannah, who plopped herself down in the tiny space alongside Button's bed, perks back up to a sit in response to some stimulus I have failed to take in. As she scans the hallway and then the room, her eyes fall on a teddy bear Button's roommate has perched on the windowsill, and she decides it is an alien from which we must be protected. The next few moments are a distraction of proving to her that the alien has already been neutralized. Hannah's insistent warning bark is enough to get a smile from Button, but not the spontaneous genuine laugh I heard just months ago. And I can see Button's fatigue now; talking and the attendant emotion has worn her out. She falls asleep, the smile fading as she does.

As Hannah and I leave Button's room, I tiptoe even though Hannah's nails click on the floor. Something makes me think of those cranes, the family flying south together. Barb pointed them out to me as Hannah and Betty tore through fallen leaves, shoving them aside with their noses as they sniffed out the tennis ball Barb had thrown for them. Even the dogs' frantic scrabbling through the dry leaves hadn't overcome the calls of the birds, they were that constant, that loud, sounding for all the world like geese. The parent pipers had been at the head of the V calling their young to follow. The young answered even as the parents called again and they answered again, the family keeping up a continuous antiphon of call, answer, call, answer: *where are you? I am here, where are you? I am here.* "*Where are you?*" Button calls, and the answer is a silence.

Follow the money has become an axiomatic phrase in American society. This almost never involves following it to a nursing home, and I find myself wondering more and more often if this is why certain residents virtually never have visitors. I think of Liz, how every time we see her she complains of being penniless. Money is power: another American axiom. Residents who perceive themselves as having no money seem to fixate on the lack because it is symbolic of autonomy. Even though no one is going hungry or unclothed, no one, in fact needs that pizza Liz longs to be able to order, being unable to satisfy a pepperoni craving leaves her feeling trapped, vulnerable, hopeless. More than once, Liz has told me that residents often hound other residents for cigarettes. "Why can't they get their own?" I asked. She explained that often their children manage the money and simply don't want their parents smoking, so won't give them cigarettes or the money to get someone else to make the purchase for them.

More residents than not are here on Medicaid, often having "spent down" their estates although Medicaid provides that assets cannot have been transferred as gifts within three years of Medicaid eligibility. In Button's case, she's done what I know others do, which is to hide money with an adult child or relative, money that subsequently disappears. Matthew, the social worker, tells me that Medicaid patients are allotted forty dollars a month spending money, but when adult children manage their parents' money, they can choose not to give the resident cash, but to bring (or not!) the personal items the resident asks for.

Another pattern seems to occur when a resident had been giving or "loaning" money out of his or her Social Security check, or providing a place to stay or care for a grandchild. When the resident is no longer able to do that (because, for example, the Social Security check goes to the nursing home facility), the family disappears. Hannah and I swing by to see Theresa after we leave Button, and immediately hear about this dimension.

Theresa is up, in her wheelchair and out in the common area, where the Fire Engine Lady snores in a beanbag seat on the floor. Today is only the second time she's been up after spending seventy-four days in bed, Theresa tells me. She's had pneumonia. "It's so good to be up," she smiles when we greet her. "That hospital really got to me. I didn't know anyone and I thought I was going to die. Well, the doctor said he almost lost me. They all thought I was going to die."

She has aged since I saw her last. A shapeless once-white blouse and gray sweatpants. Gray hair, kinked by an old, outgrown perm, brushed back and bobby-pinned off her face. Battered sneakers. Her legs are still paralyzed, she says, but she can move her arms. Yes, she has MS, they're pretty sure, but the doctor won't certify it so she still can't get therapy.

And no, nobody came to see her in the hospital as she lay dying, nor since she's been brought back. "No, I haven't seen either of my daughters in months," she says. Then she gives a little laugh. "The last time Mindy came, she asked me for money. Once she figured out that no, I really don't have any, well, she hasn't been back since. Most likely, she told the other one. But that one stays away anyway because of when I said the baby was mine. But I did used to give her money, too, when I kept the baby. To help her get on her feet, you know."

To be sure, not all the residents say things like this, but a shocking number do. And maybe it's not always accurate, but rather the simple feeling of aged people too much alone and wondering why. What I know for sure, though, is that many residents attribute their family's neglect to their own lack of money and that the impression goes uncorrected. These residents aren't senile or demented; they may be lonely and powerless, but they still have their own perceptions.

"My brother called me from down south," Theresa says. "He told me if he ever saw one of my girls on the street he'd beat her up. He even asked me if I wanted him to come up here to do it. I told him don't bother. You'd just go to jail and that wouldn't help me." She smiles and says, "Hannah's such a sweet dog. I used to be afraid of dogs, you know, but I'm not afraid of her. Anyway, it's people I should have been afraid of all along."

"It's people I should have been afraid of all along," Theresa said. Indeed. The very next week, immediately after Thanksgiving when we drop in to see Button, I am confronted with just how accurate that can be, even in this protected environment. She is crying again.

"What's wrong, Button?" I ask it hesitantly, knowing how much was already wrong and that it may not be something new or different.

She shakes her head two or three times, as if to indicate that she can't or doesn't want to talk about it. I pat the bed and Hannah, who's just learning about this, jumps up alongside Button. She kisses Button's neck, lets her own neck be hugged as Button buries her face in her fur, then she quietly stretches her length along Button's body with her head tucked in the crook of Button's elbow.

I sit down, then, and pick up her other hand, intending to just let her take comfort from Hannah as I know she does, but she launches the story after all, reiterating that I mustn't tell anyone "in authority."

"Rodney still owed me some money, and one of our daughters, you remember, it's Veronica, well, she brought me three hundred dollars in a bank envelope. I was hurting real bad, and the doctor said I could have one of them skin patches for the pain. They make me real, real sleepy. I just couldn't keep my eyes open, and she said, 'Mom, you just keep this for now. I'll come back later and see what you want me to do with it.' Well, I guess I fell asleep, that three hundred dollars in that bank envelope just a-lying on my chest like this."

Button shows me how her hands had been, she thinks, laced together over her chest, the money beneath.

"When I woke up, the envelope was right there still on my chest, and the whole three hundred dollars was gone."

"Did Veronica take it back?"

Button just shakes her head over shrugging shoulders.

"When I woke up, it was just gone. Stolen."

"Are you thinking . . . Veronica? Not somebody who works here?"

"Just stolen. They called the police, but the policeman said, 'Now ma'am, you know you're not ever going to see that money again.' That's what he said. Those words." Button cries on, quietly, and I pull tissues from the box on her nightstand and tuck two into her hand.

"I'm so sorry. I'm so sorry." There is simply nothing else to say, no way to redeem it for or with her. Hannah shifts and lays her chin on Button's chest, as I just sit in silence for a while holding Button's hand.

Most of the time the forest is purely refuge, but sometimes, like today, it is an uncanny mirror of the human world. When Hannah and I hike with Barb and Betty in the slant light of winter's early dusk, a flock of crows repeatedly overflies us as we climb the steep hill leading to the pine Cathedral. A great horned owl hoots and Barb stands still a minute, looking up. The sky is that same deep periwinkle and the light of the sun on the upper sycamore branches makes them a startle of white against it. "Those crows are after the owl," Barb says, scanning, making an eye-shield with her hand. We are in shirtsleeves and fleece vests, it's that warm.

"You mean they'll attack it?"

"Not unless the owl is diseased. Or just too old."

15. Hannah at Home

I grew up without a dog or any other pet unless you count a succession of soon-dead turtles and goldfish. Once my father accidentally uncovered the nest of three baby chipmunks while digging in the backyard. He built a wire cage, and they were going to be my pets until I learned that chipmunks have a mean bite and don't fetch well. We released them into the woods within a week. I think Dad was trying to make it up to my sister and me that we couldn't have a dog by edict from Headquarters (a.k.a. Mom), who was adamant on the subject. "I'm allergic. You're allergic. They're dirty. It would bite you. It would bite me." Pick a reason, any reason, and she issued it, her tone that of a General handing down orders. My mother is, simply put, not a dog person. But recessive dog-loving, dog-needing genes must have combined in me because I haven't been without a dog since the day I was on my own. And Hannah is the best of that thirty-year history. Simply put and without using the word lightly or easily, I love her.

It's a love that has grown with her. Now, in December, when the earth should be flattening its ears for winter, I remember last year and how the weather lost track of time then, too, and Indian summer slipped into December. It rained all the time for weeks before Hardy had the emergency bypass surgery, and the still-warm ground was saturated as it is now. Hannah's unauthorized forays into the woods after deer lasted longer and frightened me more. It's easiest to remember the stages of her training when I envision her in the context of the changing woods. At the nursing home, time blurs into a uniformity of temperature (hot) and scenery (sterile except for cardboard cut-out holiday decorations) and her development gets lost against that backdrop.

Now she almost always comes readily, even out in the woods, even when she's flushed some deer. Sometimes it takes a loud whistle, sometimes two of them, but within a minute I'll hear her crashing back through the underbrush. When she reaches the trail above or below me, she gallops to me, puts the brakes on at the last minute and slides to a panting halt, knowing full well there's a treat waiting in my hand. She still has a lot of puppy in her. Whenever Alan or I come home, Hannah greets us ecstatically, a present, one of her cherished toys, always in her mouth, her whole back half swaying in a wild, playful wag. But she rarely empties all the wastebaskets in the house anymore, nor rummages for sacrifices the house might make to the Retaliation Diet when she's left alone.

As she's matured, we've continued to work on obedience skills and she's continued to develop a will of her own. Adolescence. I've raised two children; how could I have forgotten the pleasure of that? We've kept working with a training collar and lead, especially because heel is such an important command in the nursing home as we make our way through the corridors. Interestingly, though, it's there that she heels best and responds instantly to come, almost as if she understands that she's working, and the stakes are higher. It's something like the amazement of having your children use good manners when your in-laws are visiting, even though other nights you're picking spaghetti off the walls and breaking up milk-snorting contests.

I'm also finding that Hannah distinguishes between residents and staff. When a staff member who's a "dog person" lights up at the sight of Hannah and talks to her, she's still fairly likely to dart over, go up on her hind legs and lap out a quick face wash. Interestingly, she never does this with residents except by specific verbal and non-verbal permission. She knows Connie loves it, and Connie's an exception, but even when a resident is patting his or her lap signaling Hannah to put her front paws up, she'll check my face first for confirmation that it's all right. Lately, I've been having her get up on Button's bed and stretch out alongside Button's body simply because Button wants it, but I notice Hannah's hesitation, her need for extra confirmation that this is really what I mean for her to do. I think I know why.

The very first night I brought Hannah home, we'd already set up a bed for her on the floor next to me. She was wrought up in puppy excitement as she toured the house, and when we got to the bedroom she covered the carpet in one bound and leapt onto the bed. Alan and I simultaneously shouted "Off!" because I do have allergies and even if I didn't, the bed isn't big enough for the three of us. She instantly complied. I've always felt a little badly about it because I know we frightened her. For a year she didn't get on the bed at all.

Until the day last summer when a headache had had Alan in a vice grip for twenty-four hours. Delta Society training material suggests direct physical contact with an animal can lower blood pressure and reduce pain, so when Alan finally gave in and laid down, I used treats to coax Hannah up beside him. Several hours later he got up having slept deeply and without pain. Alan was amazed and if I hadn't already believed the Delta Society and Therapy Dogs International, I did then. Now we've reached compromise. Hannah's invited onto the bed before we go to sleep if we're reading or watching television; when we turn off the light to sleep, she jumps down onto her own bed alongside ours and stays there. It's become part of her ongoing training to get on the bed and stretch out along a resident's leg with her head at his or her waist, and then get back down immediately when signaled to leave.

Every now and then I am fearful around Hannah, but it's my fault, not hers when I instinctively tense in a situation that would have provoked a snap from our cockapoo who'd have eagerly bitten a person as a T-bone steak. But I've never once seen any indication that Hannah even knows how to snap or would consider learning. She approaches all humans with eager love, unrestrained and un-constrained. (And other animals for that matter, including the mole she caught in the yard, brought in and tenderly deposited, still very much alive, on the kitchen floor, probably expecting us to feed and shelter it even though the little bugger and all his relatives need their own zip code for the village they've founded in our yard.) What I've finally come to is a recognition that I trust her, the sort of bedrock trust that's rare and precious whether it exists between two humans or one human, one dog.

Hannah lives to play, to eat, and for her daily hikes which are usually in the late afternoon when my day's work is drawing to a more or less satisfactory close. If I'm at the computer when she decides she's been patient long enough, she'll sit at my elbow and hold me in an intent and guilt-provoking stare. Her ears go up and she stands at rigid attention when one of us opens the closet in which her trail toys are kept, and when I'm actually tying hiking shoes on, she erupts frenetic anticipation. On the trail, she'll chase and retrieve anything that's thrown in any direction, of course, but the "kong on a rope" toy is arguably her favorite. A hard rubber gizmo, indestructible, in the shape of a rounded pyramid, a rope emerging from the center by which a person can fling it twice as far as his or her tennis ball range, the kong-on-a-rope has this additional magnificence: it floats, thanks to a foam insert.

In fact, there's a whole little story about Hannah and her kongs. That's plural because she's probably had a total of fifteen in the past year alone, quite an impressive tally for an indestructible toy. She lost a few in the woods while on unauthorized forays. One or two might have been caught in the upper reaches of trees thanks to a poorly aimed throw; Hardy's arm is infamous. One kong lived for months wrapped around a telephone wire in my neighborhood, Alan's personal humiliation. Most, however, died in one of the relentless tugs of war between Hannah and Betty during which neither dog will give up so the kong finally does. The rope pulls out and both dogs fly backward.

We took to buying them in bulk, sharing the cost with Barb and Hardy. Hannah and Betty refined their war maneuvers as the ammunition supply increased and soon a new kong would last less than half a hike. It was, in short, getting very expensive. All of us studied kong construction, then considered buying massive amounts of stock in the kong company but finally concluded that we'd have to switch to another toy albeit one less beloved by our dogs.

Nothing held up any better than the kong, though. In desperation, I called Bark Harbor, a wonderful canine specialty store in Bar Harbor, Maine, that Alan and I had stumbled on last summer on our way home from Nova Scotia. I explained the dilemma to Jim Smith, owner and evident toy expert who'd first impressed us enormously by selling us Hannah's "baby," a stuffed bear with a squeaker imbedded, the only one Hannah's had and still has in which the squeaker hasn't ended up both dead and separated from the body of the toy, stuffing strewn around the house, within ten minutes. It was clear to us the man knows dogs.

"No toy will withstand two Labs in a tug-of-war," Jim said. "I'm guessing you've got a head whipper."

"Oh do we ever." Indeed, Hannah's style involves a deadly trick. She braces her feet, shifts her weight to her back end and shakes her head violently side to side while maintaining the steady backward pressure. Betty, on the other hand, hunches her shoulders slightly and hunkers down with a steady, immovable cast-in-cement determination that the head whipper isn't going to whip *her* head. The war used to involve a huge kong throw into Big Pond or Harker's Run, a race to retrieve it with the dog who didn't get there first grabbing the trailing rope for a tandem swim to wherever it was shallow enough to start the tug-of-war for final possession and the right to present it to the human thrower. Battles were declared a draw when the rope flew loose of the kong and both dogs would drop their pieces in disgust after tumbling over backward.

What Jim did was give me elaborate instructions on how to do kong repair, which involved needle-nosed pliers, plastic boat rope, matches to sear off the end fibers, extra cotton rope to make a hand-friendly throwing loop. We had a significant supply of old, ropeless kongs and Alan set out to develop a prototype Lab-proof floating kong on a rope. I've known him to chortle over this for hours, smug in his superiority as he breeds ever-more elaborate kongs, designed for the distance throw into water, a quick pop-up into a float, and confident ability to withstand the head whip vs. the plant-and-pull.

The kong wasn't the first toy Hannah's been able to sideline. We can't afford to let her play with her true obsession too often, however, because it requires a completely empty field at least the size of a football stadium.

The Red Ball. I have virtually never seen a creature, human or animal, be so in love, so utterly out-of-control—obsessed with anything. I am in awe of her passion. It's soccer-ball sized, made of very hard plastic, surprisingly heavy, and my dog flips out at the sight of it. Sold as a ground toy, it's supposed to be impossible for a dog to pick up in its teeth and it's too large and heavy to retrieve anyway. Supposed to be, at least, and at first it was.

The first time Hannah even saw it, she went nuts. Using her back legs as springs, she leapt into the air when Alan instinctively raised it over his head while issuing the suddenly useless Off! command.

Hannah had gone stone deaf. She just kept leaping, throwing herself against his body, intent on dislodging it from his grasp however she could. He's six feet three, but Hannah obliterated that small advantage by turning into a tornado, a *psychotic* tornado, and he fought his way to the car, flung the ball onto the floor, slammed the door and staggered backward to consider what had just happened. With the red ball out of sight, Hannah was immediately calm.

For a while, when Hannah needed an exceptionally good workout we'd take the red ball out of the trunk of the car (definitely not safe to store it anywhere in the house) and turn Hannah loose with it in an athletic field before we hit the trails. She'd use her nose and dribble it soccer-style in a mad dash from one end to the other, back and forth until we had to take it away because she was frothing at the mouth and we were afraid she'd drop dead. She'd stop, try to figure out how to get her mouth around the ball, couldn't do it, naturally, and then furiously chase it the length of the field again.

It all worked just fine. We got a good two weeks out of it. Until Hannah defeated the red ball by doing what the catalog proudly proclaimed to be impossible. She picked it up. There's one small hole in the smooth surface of the ball in which there's a single recessed screw. Aye. There's the rub. She worked and worked until she wedged one of her long canine teeth into that little hole, wore a groove into the plastic with her opposing tooth, and finally, one day, she had enough leverage to pick up the damn red ball.

Back to the drawing board. Alan stuffed the hole with plastic wood. Hannah went nuts again. And once again she found a tiny chink. Alan's now refilled that chink and is sanding the surface of the plastic wood to make it perfectly flush. We shall see who wins the next round.

My money is on Hannah.

Hannah on the bed, her body curled into Alan's as if she understood her role exactly, is one of the images of Hannah that lingers in my mind's eye, soft and lightly right in the moment like a goose-down comforter over pain. But also, the beauty of her loping, athletic run across a field, unfettered, confident, the perfect offspring of instinct and ability. The wild exultation of her splay-legged flight off the banks of Big Pond and Harker's Run, the rhythmic power of her swimming shoulders as she cuts through whatever season is mirrored on the water. And Hannah in my writing room, stretched out in the sunlight on the floor, her rich coat glossy as mink, keeping me company even now in the moment of writing about her. I get up to go put my arms around her for the in-her-sleep sigh and purr response. She rolls onto her back as I approach, stretching for the luxury of a stomach rub. Dog people will understand when I say that one of the most difficult aspects of my increasingly frequent trips to Mom and Dad's is that I can't have Hannah with me there.

At the end of the day, of course, it all circles back home, back to love. Last month, when early November rains pelted for days, Harker's Run swelled to the top of its banks, in a furious hurry to get where it was going. The water churned brown, its speed pulling silt off the bottom and eating chunks out of the land again. More big trees toppled as the land gave way.

One trail we often take edges the little river. Hannah has several swimming holes along it, pockets where—presuming the moving and pooled waters aren't shrunken by too many rainless days—the bank is high and water deep enough for the joyous splay-legged Hannah leap. I have to watch where I throw the ball. I've seen her jump into water that's dangerously shallow, although generally she seems to instinctively adjust to changing water levels. Strangers and friends, though, often gasp when they witness one of Hannah's flying leaps, sometimes from a bank eight or ten feet above the water. I admit, my heart's been in my mouth more than once.

That particular day, however, I had no such concern. The water was high, perfect for diving, and Hannah's a very strong swimmer. But I failed to factor in the effect of a second, newly downed tree, and the proximity of both to where another creek, usually too small to have ever merited a name, empties into Harker's Run.

An old downed sycamore partly submerged in the water. A newly uprooted tree falling partly over the old one, creating a triangle. Just upstream, a swollen creek emptying into the swollen little river, creating a confluence. In Canada, they call it a deadhead: converging currents plus an obstacle equal a whirlpool.

Hannah jumped in, an enormous belly-flop over the thick exposed roots on which clumps of dirt still clung. It only took a couple of seconds for me to realize something was terribly wrong. For one thing, only her nose was out of the water, instead of her whole head. For another, she didn't immediately turn downstream to make her way to the bank by swimming with the current. The current carried her backward, too strong for her to even reverse herself, to face where it was taking her and to swim with it, rather than against it.

And very quickly, faster than I could do anything but scream, it shoved her against one of the downed trees, right at the confluence, intensified as it was by the newly downed tree. She was in the middle of a deadly triangle. In another instant, she was pulled completely under, gone.

I remember shouting, "She'll die!" to Barb, who had Betty up on the bank, and scrabbling down the tangle of torn-up roots that still clung to the bank like clutching arms and hands. As soon as I was over them, I stumbled into the water, from which I had to climb onto the horizontal trunk to even get to where Hannah had gone under. The tree that trapped Hannah was protecting me from the current, but I wore heavy hiking shoes that, although they gave me the footing I needed on bank and tree-tangle, made me feel ponderously slow. I was cement-shod, awkward, desperate.

I made it onto the trunk and was trying to figure out from which side of it to go into the water; where I'd last seen Hannah, the upstream side, or to go to the other side and hope the current would work with me. I was convinced, though, that she was tangled in debris underneath the tree and that my best chance of extracting her would be from where she'd gone under. I was just reaching that upstream spot when the current spit her out, gasping and unable to swim, on the downstream side of the jam.

Barb immediately started calling Hannah, to orient her to the closest bank and safety. I clumsily splashed in on that side of the tree and half pushed, half-lifted her toward the bank. She started to climb but didn't have the strength. My shouts from behind her and Barb's from above her, along with both my hands thrusting her forward, were finally enough.

Barb's hand pulled me up and out of the water behind my dog. I got my arms around Hannah and felt her heart racing, like my own.

Once we were home, I called our vet to see if there was anything I needed to do. Mainly, I was worried that she might have water in her lungs. Dr. Reagh, though, couldn't quite get over it. "You went in the river after her?" He said it several times, as if it were an amazement. "Did you think about it first? You put yourself in harm's way."

I honestly don't think I was in any particular danger. Barb was there and she's strong, skilled and fearless. But the answer was no, I didn't particularly think about it first.

I shrugged the vet off with a rhetorical, "What else would I do?" What I meant was I love this dog. She is mine and I am hers. She and I are in it together.

16. Hope

I have a vivid memory of when I first knew I had begun to lose my parents. It was six years ago. Dad's limp was worse, he was more deaf, Mom's tremors were more profound. Alan didn't see this, though; he saw only that they were still alive, still relatively healthy, still in charge of their own lives. Somehow I knew from the set of my husband's mouth, the angle of his chin as he rested his head on the high chair-back and stared out over the water that he was thinking about his mother, and that he felt angry and alone, while my father went on, speaking of himself. "I have no idea why I'm such a lucky man. I am so blessed. So I have arthritis. So what? I can walk. Mom can walk. All we ask is that the good Lord not take us yet. *We are not ready.*"

The moment was so layered it was nearly alive with its light and shadows, the markings of low-country tides moving and revealed as the channels and basins emptied themselves. From my parents' porch, marsh and water unevenly stripe the horizon as it spreads toward the sea, like the layers of meaning and experience that mark our souls, the imperfect parallels by which we think we know one another. Alan's mother had been dead for six months. Well before she died, a stroke had stripped off an essential layer of self-awareness and control, and the dependency imposed by the still-earlier loss of an eye reared, increasingly strident and difficult. She wanted to be early everywhere, not ten or fifteen minutes early, but four, five, sometimes six hours early, and nothing could convince her that her time frame was off. She would furiously yell at a son or her husband, "You've made me late all my life and I don't see why you can't do what I want for a change." None of them had ever known she believed they had made her chronically late; none of them remembered whether there was any truth to her assertion. But she was adamant. If they didn't leave when she wanted, she would grope her blind way outside and begin to walk onto a four-lane highway, or make her way into their car—or worse, a stranger's car—and blow the horn persistently. There were dozens of other aching demands, and a crushing, comfortless depression. When God did not give her back her sight, the last of which was taken by the stroke, regardless of how much she prayed, terror and despair became her cruel, shadow-companions.

Her death wrung me with how much there is to fear: physical and mental dependency, the loss of the power of the mind, the slip-sliding away of all we've chosen our lives to stand for. Here it was again now, the looming fact that my parents' decline had begun. This was as strong and healthy as they would ever be. And I recognized that I would do anything to spare them what is to come. I would do anything to spare myself.

He loves his life, my father does. When I was in my teens and twenties, Dad used to insist, "I will never die." Then, he believed that it is the *belief* in death and its inevitability that poisons and finally does end our lives, that attitude can overcome anything. I remember vehemently arguing with him, using words like denial and repression. Now that he had begun to make reference to his eventual death, I demurred, not quite brushing aside his words, but deflecting them. When he told me that he couldn't remember what he wants for as long as it takes him to go in search of it, I laughed and told him that the same thing happens to me all the time, which, however true, was fundamentally dishonest because I knew that my experience was not the same as his, not as frightening, not heralding potential helplessness.

Nothing was all that bad yet then. It's just getting there now for Mom. How could Alan not compare, with at least regret, and perhaps outright bitterness sometimes, his parents' lives over their last two years together to those of my parents'? How could he not feel his were cheated? By the time his mother died, eighteen hours after the respirator was turned off, three days after her second, cataclysmic stroke, Alan, his brothers, and their father had endured months and months of desperation, trying to spell one another as their wife and mother could not be alone for so much as a minute, and most minutes were filled with her irrationality, her agony. Some deaths are worse, slower, rob us of our selves more surely than others.

And Alan and I both know that there are deaths far worse than his mother's. I have begun to worry about this, too. Will Mom and Dad and my sister and I pay dearly for these extra months and years, or will we be unaccountably, undeservedly helped with more graceful partings? I counsel myself to hope for readiness and for the kindness of good deaths.

The stretch of Mom and Dad's still-manicured lawn ends in the rough five foot wide fringe of spartina on either side of and beneath the dock that reaches like a hand into the narrow channel. Just beyond the mooring channel, another stretch of marsh, only mud at dead low tide, watery but clogged and still impassable at high. Beyond those, the wider water of the Intracoastal waterway, where the current of the incoming tide ripples visibly, and the sandy spit of Topsail Island. Lea Island, uninhabited now, is nearly an apparition, nearer the mainland than Topsail, but ghostly with the sagging gray remains of the one house the island's owner built there for his own seclusion, claimed by death, time, and the sea. Another hurricane will doubtless take the last of it. How utterly we finally disappear. Alan's father remarried at eighty-four and has celebrated his fourth wedding anniversary. We are all pleased, yet secretly frightened by how little and yet how greatly his mother's death has marked us all, life going on as it does.

Twilight deepens on the porch before it does over the lawn, the marshes, and the water. In the shadows, now, Mom and Dad both talk about dying, sometimes saying "if something happens to me," sometimes, striving for a matter of fact tone, saying "when." Dad has finished preparing a comprehensive list of their assets, property, insurance policies, and "instructions to survivors." I'm grateful, to be sure, and unaccountably saddened by this generous gesture.

The lit house drew my family in from dusk that evening, but I stayed outside, forcing myself to consider their absence. I changed seats to rock in Mom's chair, observing how the waterway held its memory of the parade of boats which have passed through it, cutting the surface by their coming, churning, and flattening it with their leaving. I had started to lose them.

What brings this memory so vividly to the forefront of my mind? It's something my mother says today as we're talking on the phone. She's bemoaning how much she sleeps these days, taking long morning and afternoon naps and going to bed for the night as early as eight thirty or nine. "I fall asleep at the drop of a hat," she says frequently. Before the fall that put her arm in a sling, she'd slap her hands together in a gesture to show how quickly sleep overcomes her. But then, in a rare moment of philosophical musing, today she goes on. "You know, I never used to understand how people could say they were ready to go. How could they give up their lives? But I'm starting to understand. I can tell it'll be all right for me. You get to a certain point and you think, all right, it's enough. I've had enough, done enough, felt enough, whatever. I'm ready to go. It's not that I'm exactly there yet, but I'm getting there."

When I ask her if she believes in an afterlife, my mother shrugs her shoulders. "I hope so. But in a way I doubt it. It's okay, though. It's been enough."

Now in the dead of winter, dark falls early and seals in the cold. There's not much of a snowpack, though the couple of inches on the ground have been sealed by a scrim of ice. Of course, Hannah loves it. She bursts into the cold of our hikes with total exultation, flinging herself after balls with unstoppable energy. A couple of days ago, I miscalculated that energy enough to embarrass myself on a grand scale. My first mistake was to give her the red ball, out on the playing field near the entrance to the trails, the same place she regularly breaks up organized sports by stealing the ball when she's supposed to be obediently and sedately getting into the back seat of my car.

Anyway, I did it, I gave it to her, and, predictably, she became an instant force of nature measurable with the Richter Scale. I threw the red ball out into the empty field and Hannah tore after it, executed a magnificent stop/turn, and shot back at me dribbling it expertly with her nose. My problem was I didn't move fast enough. She expected me to sidestep, I didn't make it, and I went down. Hannah hardly glanced back to see if I needed emergency medical attention. No, she dribbled that damn red ball into the parking lot behind me, across it, down into a culvert and right into a big drainage pipe. She stood there barking while I panted up behind her. Then she started into the pipe after the ball. Of course, her nose hit the ball, which rolled farther in.

"NO, girl, no. Leave it. Get out of there," I was shouting, gesticulating and, finally, on my knees reaching into the drainpipe to grab Hannah, and I was just feet from the road. Drivers were rubbernecking over their shoulders as they passed.

Hannah backed out of the pipe, probably alarmed by the ruckus I was creating. I grabbed her collar, but she wasn't about to leave the pipe's mouth, from which her beloved red ball called her.

Is there any doubt left about what came next? Picture a middle-aged woman crawling into a drainage pipe, her frantic barking Lab behind her. Picture my hips and rear protruding from the pipe. Perhaps you can even hear the honking horns. No, I couldn't extricate the red ball. But Hannah's hope has already been rewarded. I've placed a rush order for a new red ball.

The weather and hope have energized Big Sam, too. He's primed to go home. "Next Wednesday," he says. He's decided to reject meals on wheels because he'd have to be home at eleven thirty each day for the delivery and he doesn't want to be tied down. "Goodness, I say. Are you sure? Eleven thirty is fairly early; you'd have the whole rest of the day to be out picking up college girls."

"I'm getting a new car, too," he says, flipping the fleece ball into the air for Hannah who makes a straight-up vertical leap to catch it. "I can cook for myself. I like that Shake 'n Bake stuff." Understand that he's speaking to me from his wheelchair, which is parked in the exact spot it was when I first met him and where I've found him every day that I've been to Golden View for the past year. He may, in fact, be wearing the same scarlet shirt that becomes a focal point in the neutral tones of the dayroom, especially in January, when gray clouds are a ceiling just above the telephone wires outside. So what has changed that now he can go home? I'm awash in ambivalence. I could never see that Sam needed to be living here in the first place, yet I'm concerned that he does, for example, need the support of meals on wheels and senior transportation services. A new car? I worry that this may be a fantasy of hope rather than reality. It's possible he's fooling himself or the doctor, both or neither.

The issue of who, if anyone, hope is fooling brings Hannah to mind. In last week's hard rain Hannah didn't want to go outside to pee, an ironic trait for a dog I can't keep out of the river. Finally I insisted, holding a treat in my hand. Hannah hurried out several feet onto the lawn where she faked a squat that was a half-second dip, utterly unproductive, and dashed back to me expecting her treat.

"Do I look like some kind of stupid?" I sputtered. "Don't you lie to me. Get out there and pee." I swear I don't know which one of us she was fooling the first time, but she was finally resigned. Out she went where she squatted in the cold rain peppering the lawn and peed like a racehorse.

At any rate, I don't know if Big Sam is even trying to fool anyone, but we shall see. He'll have his chance to work it out, at least, and perhaps that's all any of us ever really have.

Like Big Sam, Button's notion of hope has to do with the concrete road between here and the immediate future. "I hope I get to go to Tennessee. If Leann didn't spend the money she's supposed to be keeping for me, which I think she did, I can go if the three thousand dollars I owe is paid. See, I didn't get on Medicaid quick enough, so there's this back bill. But once it's paid, I can go to the nursing home in Tennessee near my sister's." She wants out for another reason, too. The roommate she's had since the day she was brought here nearly a year ago, shortly after her husband announced he wanted to go out and "taste the world," died on Christmas Day. Pearl was a hundred and one, fragile—thin as translucent bone china, but lively minded. She and Button would watch television together and enjoy insulting the hopelessly stupid soap opera characters as much as they did the good cry they had for the beautiful victims of the hopelessly stupid. I'd been in to see Button on Christmas Eve and didn't even recognize Pearl; I'd thought Button had a new roommate, that's how quickly (mercifully!) Pearl had deteriorated from the always-dressed (complete with necklace and earrings) tiny woman in a wheelchair with a purse on her lap, to a toothless skeleton blindly groping for Button's hand. Their beds had been pushed together as if to make one king-sized one. "She just always wanted me to hold her hand. I'd stroke it and she'd calm down. I knew the day she was dying, I knew it. All the signs came back from when my son died of cancer. I was with him then, stroking his hand just the same way."

A chapter about hope may not be the best place for the remainder of this story, but I'm going to tell it. I'll tell it because one of the things I hope for my parents, my husband, myself, my children, and friends is the gift of a good death, one attended lovingly, reassuringly as Button did Pearl's. I also hope my dog will be on my bed with me, and that, should it be in a nursing facility, whomever I live with will mourn and be helped in that mourning. Here, it was Button who put on the call-light to let the nurse know, at one thirty in the morning, that Pearl's heart had finished twenty-seven small last thumps beneath Button's hand, laid on her friend's chest when she heard the rattling last breaths. As usual, no one answered the call right away, Button says. And when someone finally came, followed by belatedly bustling attendants with a body bag, no one held Button's hand as she heard the zipper through the curtain abruptly drawn by attendants between Button's and Pearl's abruptly moved-apart beds.

I do hear, in certain residents, that shift from hoping to go home to hoping for a good death. And there's a real difference between the wanting to die that's a symptom of depression and the kind that signals the readiness to let go of life that accompanies acceptance and relative peace with what has come and gone. I hear it most often in the nonagenarians whose health has deteriorated but whose minds are quite present, those who aren't so much tired of living but more finished with it. Their families may be terribly sad, but the dying individual is less so, except as they watch their sons and daughters suffer the losing process. I'm guessing it may be that way for Clare down the road. Already she's largely achieved a truce with MS.

For the most part, though, "my" residents—*Hannah's* residents— aren't there. If they see no hope of leaving the facility, they tend to be otiose and depressed as Mary is, except when Hannah's with her. Mary's desire to die is no grateful expression of "it's been enough," but rather one of despair. If they do hope to leave, they fixate on it without much regard for the degree of realism attached to the dream. Like Big Sam, perhaps. His plans for being "sprung" seem realistic on one hand, but when he starts talking about how he doesn't need meals on wheels or senior transportation services, well, I'm far less sure.

Liz, however, is another matter entirely. She's pitching a tennis ball for Hannah out in the courtyard as she describes "what they're doing with me."

"I feel like I'd do best just getting my own apartment here and going back to work at K-Mart. They know I'm really good at helping customers there, and I know they'd hire me right back."

"So . . . is that what you're doing?"

Liz makes the mistake of pausing to answer me, and Hannah leaps to snatch the ball out of her upraised hand. She immediately drops it at Liz's feet and barks, to make sure Liz gets it. Hey, this is *my* time. Play with *me*. More and more, Hannah distinguishes between residents and "regular" people. She doesn't make demands on residents, but waits for cues. Liz, interestingly enough, she treats entirely differently, nosing for attention and play right away. I take it as an assessment: this one's all right, I don't have to take care of *her*.

And Hannah's right. Liz knows exactly how to handle her, which none of the other residents do, nor does Hannah make them have to.

"Hey, girl, just a minute now." Liz picks up the ball, tells Hannah to sit, and then just holds the ball and answers me while Hannah waits impatiently.

"My kids are still my guardians and they want me to go to a women's recovery place for something like six months first." She makes a moue, obviously displeased with the turn of events. She's cut her hair again (and managed to sneak another color job on it when David was on duty for the weekend, correctly figuring that, being male, he'd not notice). It's a dark brunette shining in the cold sun. Her coat is old, third-hand appearing, blah-colored with one pocket partly torn off, and the reason, she says, she didn't want to come out when I suggested it. But I want her to feel the outside world, breathe crisp new air, so I told her Hannah needed an outdoor break before seeing more of her people.

"Maybe that's a good thing?"

"Well, I don't want to. But yeah, I suppose it *could.*"

"After all you've been through, maybe that's a way to take your life back one step at a time rather than all at once."

"I won't know anybody."

"True. But look at what you've done here, met everyone, become everyone's friend. And helped so many. Have you ever thought of working in a nursing home?"

"Actually, I sort of have. Maybe in Activities . . ."

"Liz, you'd be wonderful at that. You have a gift with older people, you know now what makes a difference in a nursing home, and you know what residents *feel* like. What a unique perspective."

"Oh yeah. I sure do. I like helping the people here. Some of them ask for me—when the staff try to do something with them, they'd rather have *me*." Indeed, I've seen Liz at bingo, running cards for four or five residents at once. They *do* ask for her. And she took over caring for a beta fish I brought to a totally disabled patient who desperately wanted a pet.

"You could be the one who gets in there and pushes for animals and plants and fish and interesting things to do. And maybe even decision making!" My tone mocks the last part, as if to say, *what a concept!*

Liz is looking very interested.

"How about I get you some literature about facilities that do that? In case you do go into this as a career. Instead of Kmart, I mean."

Liz laughs, then turns serious. "Do you really think I'd be good at it?"

It's such a pleasure to be able to give a spontaneous, truthful answer. "I absolutely do. And for heaven's sake, get a dog, get her trained, and take her to work with you!"

"That I'll do for sure," she says, and turns to Hannah whose eyes are riveted on the ball tantalizing her from Liz's palm. "I may just have to get a chocolate Lab like you, girl." She pitches the ball overhand, a strong throw that sends Hannah flying across the enclosed quadrangle. From behind the glass doors, Big Sam watches in his wheelchair, obscured by reflected sunlight almost as if underwater. But I can make out his wistful smile as Hannah skids on a pebbled area, snatches the ball on a bounce, and trots back onto the grass, her tail a triumphant flag.

A couple of weeks after Button reiterates her hope to make it to Tennessee, she is bright with another hope. It turns out that Button really might make it out, but for the most unlikely of reasons. She has a gentleman caller. Harold. And he's been coming "right regular."

He's been her friend for years and years. Rodney, she tells me, used to resent him "something fierce," although Harold was his friend too and came to visit when Rodney was home. "I always knew he liked me," Button says softly, a smile teasing at her mouth, eyes shyly downcast.

"Hmmm. Had a thing for you did he? You hot number, you."

Button's chin comes up and she erupts in open laughter. "Yep. And had it pretty good, I'd say."

She'd liked him too, but "I was in love with Rodney, don't you know. I wasn't interested in no one else."

Now she is, though. Now she's *very* interested. Harold's coming to call. Not only that, he's talking about getting married. To Button. And bringing her to his house, his *ranch* house where everything is, or shortly will be, handicapped accessible.

Yesterday, at year's end, thick wet snow fell all day, frosting each separate pine bough, branch and twig in the woods. Hannah and Betty romped, exhilarated by the cold. There's ice partway across Harker's Run now, but still patches of open water. Betty will run along the bank until she finds them and crosses there, but Hannah will scamper over any ice that will hold her as if to say, "Oh quit being such a wimp." There is some danger, though, of course, and we try to direct Hannah to follow Betty's lead. *Fat chance*, her dashing rump wags the message back at me.

Consistently, though, Hannah finds her own way. And the forest hides such beauty in this season dreaded by so many. What I've learned with and from my dog in a year here, as in the nursing home where Hannah and I share the winter of so many lives, is that there *can* be less to fear than I thought. Whatever connects us to the natural world and to each other is an antidote to powerlessness and despair. I've learned that nurturing is as essential to the giver as to the recipient and that it empowers us in a transcendent and mysterious way. Lift a fledgling bird in your hand and release it skyward; our always-fledgling spirits will fly with it. Creative nurturing can take place anywhere and, it turns out, is always mutual no matter how it begins: with residents, with staff, with a loving Labrador retriever. Children, goldfish, birds, mother cats and their litters, tulips, tomato plants. Anything counts, everything matters.

There are innumerable ways we can allow, enable, and encourage people to keep nurturing. We *need* them to keep nurturing. I have to accept Helen's offers to let Hannah out when Alan and I aren't home rather than seek out the twelve-year-old across the street, thinking I'm sparing her.

I can't write the end of my family's story yet. The year of this memoir has circled its tail and laid down to sleep while my parents, my sister, and I limp on from crisis to crisis. It will be that way for a while, but I need to ask Mom for her recipes and Dad how to defeat the moles in our yard that have just elected their first governor. My parents need to know that I need what they've learned and created. And I have to be honest enough to admit that I do, rather than taking refuge in the nurturing role in which I've come to feel safest and most in control. I have to be brave enough about my own future to ask them to teach me about their present experience, too.

In the section of forest Hannah and I most love, above the upstream bridge where Harker's cuts its way through a high embankment, the little river sings over and around rocky rapids made by exposed stones and snowy ice bridges between them. Each side of the bank is fringed with horsetail grass, poking out of its white comforter beneath the tall, old forest branches weighed with thick frosting. The trail has disappeared entirely now but beneath the snow sleep the wildflowers, and Hannah runs on.

Epilogue

Between the writing and the publication of this book, my mother died quite suddenly at home, Dad alone by her side. My father had continued to take care of her without outside help, "just doing my job," he says. She had finally adjusted to using a walker, too, in spite of the fact that walkers are for old people. Now eighty-eight, Dad is carrying on strong, as healthy and rooted in place as any of the wild onions in his yard. After he mows them, he watches boats go up and down the Intracoastal Waterway from his own porch. And my sister has moved to North Carolina.

Acknowledgments

Heart thanks to Joe Mackall and Dan Lehman, editors, and the Editorial Board of *River Teeth: A Journal of Nonfiction Narrative* for honoring the book with the River Teeth Literary Nonfiction Prize. Any author knows the pole vault they have given my spirit and work. Joe Mackall offered invaluable editorial guidance prior to publication, and I especially thank him for that. Much appreciation goes to the staff of the University of Nebraska Press for bringing the book into being, and doing it beautifully. I am especially indebted to Ladette Randolph and Sandra Johnson and to copyeditor Timothy Schaffert.

Nancy Fox, executive director of the Eden Alternative, and Sandy Ransom, RN, MSHP, director of the Texas Long Term Care Institute gave helpful information and support. Thanks also to Sydney Lea for permission to quote from his poem "Annual Report," which appears in *No Sign* (copyright 1987, University of Georgia Press), and to J. C. and Rhondal Rupel, and the staff of the Oxford Copy Shop.

A lived life, funneled and squeezed out in words, like frosting onto a cake though occasionally less sweet, resulted in this book. Barbara Eshbaugh lived it with me, read the first version of the manuscript, and introduced me to the Eden Alternative concept. Hardy Eshbaugh taught me the names of all the flowers in the forest (even the ones I get wrong). I am grateful to my neighbor of a quarter-century, who generously allowed me to relate aspects of her story. Anna Tuttle Villegas, wise first reader, said to suck it up and be brave enough to talk about myself and my family, too. Debra Conner gave me her good advice, dog-devoted heart, and courage to stay the course. She is due several packages of sticky notes, a turquoise pen, and many hours. My husband, Alan deCourcy, always provides the best proofreading, rescue for the technologically impaired, good humor, dog training, kong repair, and love.

I believe my parents' strength and example is evident. This is an intimate story, and one I hope reveals their great dignity. May the apple not fall far from the tree! I am grateful for the privilege of the telling and for my sister, Jan Fuller.

I rub behind Hannah's ears and whisper *good girl, good girl*. She'd as soon have an extra treat. Or two. She gets them.

Five Shades of Shadow
Tracy Daugherty

The Untouched Minutes
Donald Morrill

*Where the Trail Grows Faint: A Year
in the Life of a Therapy Dog Team*
Lynne Hugo